The
Waiting
Years

LOUISIANA STATE UNIVERSITY PRESS / BATON ROUGE

The
Waiting
Years

⋈ BLYDEN JACKSON

Essays on
American Negro
Literature

Copyright © 1976 by Louisiana State University Press
All rights reserved
Manufactured in the United States of America

Designer: Dwight Agner
Type face: Linofilm Baskerville
Typesetter: Kingsport Press, Inc.
1977 printing

Grateful acknowledgment is hereby made for permission to reprint portions of this book which originally appeared in the following publications:

Phylon, XII (Fourth Quarter, 1950), for "An Essay in Criticism"; Journal of Negro Education (Winter, 1946), for "Largo for Adonais"; CLA Bulletin, IX (Spring, 1955), for "The Ring and the Book"; CLA Journal, IV (September, 1960), XI (June, 1968), and XII (June, 1969), for "The Negro's Image of His Universe as Reflected in His Fiction," "A Word About Simple," and "Richard Wright: Black Boy from America's Black Belt and Urban Ghettos," respectively; Michigan Quarterly Review, LXI (Spring, 1955), for "The Case for American Negro Literature"; Southern Literary Journal (Spring, 1971), for "Richard Wright in a Moment of Truth"; Journal of Negro History, LVIII (January, 1973), for "A Review of J. L. Dillard's Black English"; Rutgers University Press, for "The Minstrel Mode," from Louis D. Rubin, Jr., ed., The Comic Imagination in American Literature (New Brunswick, N.J.: Rutgers University Press, 1973); Everett/ Edwards, Inc., Deland, Florida, for "Harlem Renaissance in the Twenties" and "Jean Toomer's Cane: An Issue of Genre," both published in Warren French (ed.), The Twenties: Fiction, Poetry and Drama; National Council of Teachers of English, for "The Ghetto of the Negro Novel: A Theme with Variations," from The Discovery of English: NCTE 1971 Distinguished Lectures (Urbana, Ill.: National Council of Teachers of English, 1971), copyright © 1971 by the National Council of Teachers of English and reprinted by permission; and to College English, XXV (March, 1974), for "A Survey Course in Negro Literature," copyright © 1974 by the National Council of Teachers of English and reprinted by permission.

LIBRARY OF CONGRESS CATALOGING IN PUBLICATION DATA

Jackson, Blyden.
    The waiting years.

    Includes bibliographical references and index.
    CONTENTS: An introductory essay. —An essay in criticism. —Largo for Adonais. —The ring and the book. [etc.]
    1. American literature—Negro authors—History and criticism—Addresses, essays, lectures.
I. Title.
PS153.N5J34   810'.9'896073   74-82001
ISBN 0-8071-0173-7 (cloth)
ISBN 0-8071-0393-4 (paper)

To my wife
Roberta

Contents

An
Introductory
Essay

LOUISVILLE, Kentucky, is my hometown. I was not born there. But I was taken there so early in my childhood that my true birthplace means nothing to me. We came to Louisville — my parents, my older brother, and I — when I was not quite four. That was in the historic summer of 1914, the summer which saw the outbreak of World War I. I left Louisville, thenceforth to return only as a visitor, in the summer of 1945. Coincidence had arranged it that, as I had begun my residence in Louisville at almost the exact moment of the opening skirmishes of one of the two big wars of the century, I should withdraw from it within a short time of the closing of the second.

Presumably, anyone should get to know a town well in thirty-one years. I feel certain there was a part of Louisville that, at one time, I did know well. It could, however, only have been the Negro part. For, although Louisville was not Deep South and had, by law, only segregated schools, but no segregated public carriers (except on southbound trains), much of Louisville was not accessible to me. The municipal parks, for instance, were legally open to everyone, as was the public library, and I can distinctly recall picnicking freely in the parks when I was a little boy. But, then, by the time I was beginning to be big enough to notice girls the Park Board had built and set aside a park — Chickasaw by name (all Louisville parks had Indian names) — "especially" for the use of Negroes, so that gradually, yet rather quickly, without law, yet also with the

1

connivance of law enforcers, Chickasaw became the only park in Louisville for Negroes. In like manner, Louisville had two "colored" branch libraries, one in the west end and one in the east. All other branches were "white," as was, incidentally, the so-called main library. And I have no doubt that for many years, in the town where Fitzgerald's Jay Gatsby's Daisy Fay Buchanan and Jordan Baker passed their "beautiful white girlhoods together," any Negro so unresponsive to the community ethos as to have insisted (and he would have had to insist) upon availing himself of the services at a "white" public library, had he refused to be cozened by the usual supposedly polite deterrents, might well (I speak almost seriously now) have ended up hanging from a tree.

Yet lynching was not actually a way of life in the Louisville of my youth. Boys had gangs in those days, too, although not by any means the ferocious kind of combat groups one reads and hears about in current reports descriptive of the inner cities of our present neo-Gothic urban scene. Our gangs were more innocent and considerably less lethal, much closer in what we did and in the bucolic simplicities with which we thought to Tom Sawyer and his friends than to the warring factions of *Westside Story*. Even so, our little band of amateur commandos fitfully pursued for two or three years a modest vendetta with a white gang, the members of which lived in a neighborhood contiguous to ours. I cannot say that the white gang and ours ever had a "rumble" in what has now become the classic sense. But both of our gangs lost no opportunity to exchange insults and to taunt each other. Once or twice, when it could not be avoided, we exchanged blows. That was all there ever was to it, however—boyish bravado and high jinks; and only once can I recall that an agitated parent, who did happen to be white, appealed to the police to curb our violence. In that case, moreover, the police did not act as if we small blacks had committed a desecration of some First Commandment in laying our sooty hands rudely on our "equisized" white peers. They cautioned all the parents. I heard, or rather overheard, their conversation with my mother. It bordered on the conciliatory.

Such was the prescribed Louisville way. In my Louisville, while it was understood that Negroes had a place and should be kept therein, it was also understood that Louisville was a better than average town where ugly, brutal, open, racial friction was not the accepted thing. The local mores did not countenance the savagery of hicks. Louisville's vaunted public image could not abide such gaucherie. And so most of the "correction" of Negroes in my Louisville was perpetrated in ways that would not trespass against an ostensible observance of piety and good taste. Once on an Elysian summer evening I was strolling home in Louisville through a middle-class, white residential district. I was in my teens. A small white boy, hardly old enough to pronounce his own name—and to whom I was certainly a total stranger—alone on what I took to be his family's front lawn, hissed at me as I passed, "Nigger, nigger, nigger!" I wondered half-sardonically who his parents were. Surely they must have been responsible for training him to call me "Nigger." But where were they from that they had failed to train him not to let me hear him say it?

That was my Louisville. W. E. B. DuBois once spoke of the life of the American Negro, and the limitations imposed upon it, as a life within a veil. Perhaps nowhere in America did his words ring truer than in Louisville, at least in Louisville when I was there. Through a veil I could perceive the forbidden city, the Louisville where white folks lived. It was the Louisville of the downtown hotels, the lower floors of the big movie houses, the high schools I read about in the daily newspapers, the restricted haunts I sometimes passed, like white restaurants and country clubs, the other side of windows in the banks, and, of course, the inner sanctums of offices where I could go only as an humble client or a menial custodian. On my side of the veil everything was black: the homes, the people, the churches, the schools, the Negro park with Negro park police. By the time I was in my second year of high school even the police who patrolled the streets in which I felt at ease were black. Whatever liberties my boyhood gang had taken, as a maturing citizen no longer a boy, I was generously injected with the mumbo-jumbos of American color caste. I knew that there were two Louisvilles and, in America, two Americas. I knew, also, which of the two Americas was mine. I knew there were things I was not supposed to do, honors I was not supposed to seek, people with whom I could have been congenial to whom I was never supposed to speak, and even thoughts I could have harbored that I was never supposed to think. I was a Negro. An act of God had circumscribed my life.

Except, of course, I never thought it was an act of God. I thought both of the disparate Louisvilles and all of America that clamored so for color caste could be traced back, not to divine intervention, but to sordid human purposes and drives. As such, I thought, and still think, that both of the Louisvilles, as well as any and all Americas, were, and are, subject to change. I did not think a significant change would come easily or soon. Too much was involved. But I did think that it would come. In the meantime I was not loitering dolefully outside the white folks' barred enclosure, too immobilized by self-pity to live a life of my own. I was in no way a casualty of war.

Some years ago indeed, there was a newspaper columnist, one of the most widely read in America, Westbrook Pegler, who had grounded his reputation on antiliberal tirades. He wrote of Communists as if they were the slimiest of devils from hell, of liberals as if they were Communists, and of Negroes as if they were beneath his scorn. And then a moment came in his professional pursuits when, for a period of days—during, I think, a presidential campaign, and on, I also think, one of the campaign trains—he was thrown into close contact with some Negro newsmen. One can imagine Pegler and those newsmen in the club car of their train between working hours, almost surely as the whiskey flowed and thawed them out, peering into each others' lives. At any rate, out of the experience Pegler produced one of his most famous columns, one that began, "If I were a Negro, I would live in a state of constant fury." Yet most Negroes do not live in states of constant fury. Most Negroes in America have managed to survive, and even multiply (four and a half million at Emancipation; almost twenty-five million today), as fairly well-balanced and reasonably self-gratified individuals. It is not that Negroes are ignorant of, or unperturbed by, all that Pegler came to know and feel. But there is more to black America than a history of oppression, and more to being Negro than merely hating, or envying, whites.

I had fun in the Louisville that I knew, fun in the best of senses. It has long been incumbent upon me, as a teacher of literature, to try to immerse myself in the experience of others. Writer after writer whom I have studied has been like a conductor or a guide, who has, in the manner of Dante's Virgil, led me into, and often through, a world that was not my own. I have wanted to know intimately what Milton's world was like, or Keats's, or Melville's, or F. Scott Fitzgerald's, not to mention, since I teach Negro literature also, the worlds of Frederick Douglass or Claude McKay.

There was a time, for instance, when I projected a master's thesis on Thomas More. And so I amassed and organized, for myself, More's world, item after item, circumstantial detail after circumstantial detail. I knew who Archbishop (later Cardinal) Morton was, and John Colet, and Linacre, and, of course, Erasmus. I knew of More's tutelage in Morton's household, of his studies in the law, of the great fondness Henry VIII once professed for More, of More's family and More's favorite daughter, Meg, of the Rastells, and More's wearing of the hairshirt with which he mortified his flesh. I turned, that is, to the world of early Tudor England, to steep myself in it, almost to live in it, to know what *it* was like, so that when I would read, as I did, of Henry VIII, the monarch, boating down the Thames to steal in upon More in the privacy of More's Chelsea garden, the words in a book would no longer be mere words to me, but all would have a meaning, for me, of concrete facts actually endowed with literal reality within my field of physical perception. What I was doing was not rare. Students of literature have been doing it for centuries. It is their custom to resurrect the worlds of the writers whose works they read. But this interest of mine in writers' actual lives, this old habit of my trade, has cast its light upon my life in Louisville.

Some of the people I knew there made their marks upon a larger stage. Whitney Young was from a family associated with Louisville. I went to school with an aunt of Julian Bond and played sometimes in the street before the house of the poet Joseph Seamon Cotter. But with or without celebrities, my Louisville was a strong and rich community. I have never felt cheated because I grew up in it. It had one high school, and I still wonder if any high school anywhere ever had a better faculty. The two women who taught me Latin taught me Latin. They did not only make their classes translate. A Caesar of flesh and blood was given to me by the first of them; and the other, an old maid, gave me a Dido and Aeneas, as well as an Anchises and a host of deities and mortals, who were at least at one time bright and vivid, not at all ridiculous or trivial in my mind. The dullest of my history teachers knew her history. The best, my father, dramatized the past as if it were a play being performed before his students' eyes. The man who taught me trigonometry and college algebra, and coached me in my graduation speech, left me forever contemptuous of mental indolents who alibi that mathematics is either arid or obscure. And I still think that I am an English teacher because I once studied English under one of my high-school English teachers. Moreover, I believe my high school was as it was because my Louisville was what it was. It was the truest democracy I have ever known. I do not mean that it was perfect. But I do mean that when I have compared it with other worlds I have observed or studied, such as those I read about in my trade, no matter how exemplary the other worlds have been considered, I have never been able to bring myself to feel that life in any of those other worlds would have been better for me than life as I knew it in Negro Louisville, or that in any of those other worlds would the people I encountered have been of a nobler breed than those with whom I did consort as I grew up in Louisville.

I have taken, for example, more interest, perhaps, in Thornton Wilder's *Our Town* than I might have were I not so involved as I am in my comparison of communities. Clearly Grover's Corners in New Hampshire, the town of *Our Town*, and a citadel of Aryanism, is a paean to the best in the New England village. I empathize with Emily Webb when she realizes, from beyond the grave, how wonderful, taken for granted and unappreciated as they tended to be, were all the days there. I admit, moreover, Grover's Corners' saltiness of earth. But had I had to choose between Grover's Corners and my Louisville I would have taken Louisville. I would never have traded my parents for Emily Webb's, nor my close associates and relatives, including my cousin who went to jail, for the people that she knew. Indeed, if the intention of American color caste was (as it surely was) to make me feel abased or to induce in me that chronic state of black rage which two young black psychiatrists, confirming Westbrook Pegler, have written a book to say is a medical fact for the American Negro—then color caste, at least in my personal reaction to it, has failed. All that I need to do is remember Grover's Corners. I know, that is, as I might well depose in a court of law on my solemn oath, of at least one segregated black community, ordained and ostracized by color caste, that I would match—virtue for virtue, as well as failing for failing (because, for every Thomas More, nature seems impartially to provide a Wolsey or a Thomas Cromwell)—with the finest of white communities. I know also, incidentally, from my youth and young manhood, of some other Negro communities that I would esteem as highly as I esteem the Louisville I remember not with loathing, but with love.

I would not be so silly as to argue that segregation has not deprived Negroes. In an America without color caste Booker T.

Washington, for example, might well have become president. He was, after all, a master politician, perhaps the best of southern vintage since the Civil War. But Washington was a member of a downtrodden minority. He did belong to a people who, during his lifetime, in America were universally Jim Crowed, widely disfranchised, and frequently imposed upon (with no hope of redress) by the most inconsequential of whites. Only recently has the southern Negro sharecropper ceased to be the likeliest symbol for the most wretched of Americans. And even today, *disadvantaged* remains largely a code word, and something of a palliative, for black. Yet, my Louisville did exist, substantially as I have said it was. I have not created it out of whole cloth, nor have I taken a fantasy and tried to beguile myself and others into believing that the fantasy is true. What I have asserted as there, was there—every distinctive portion of it. And, being there, it taught me, at a time when all my basic views were acquiring what is probably their final form, the folly, as well as the iniquity, of color caste. Surely there must have been, I could hardly fail to note conclusively, something mad about a system from which everybody lost. "Deprive yourself," that system said to me. But what about the whites? I thought, when I meditated upon the Louisville that I had known —the one I had found not traumatic and depressing, but a source of much splendor and delight to a growing boy—that the whites were depriving themselves of something, too.

I finished high school in 1925. I was fourteen, and so I lectured, at my commencement, to an indulgent audience of my elders, on "Eternal Peace." In the fall I went off to college, to Wilberforce University in Ohio, three miles from Xenia and about the same distance from Yellow Springs. It was a Negro school, considerably more a Negro school than schools like Fisk, Howard, Hampton, and Tuskegee. For it had been founded by the largest of the Negro Methodist denominations, the AMEs (African Methodist Episcopal Church). It had no white patron saints in its background, no tradition of Yankee schoolmarms from Down East, no ties with the Freedmen's

Bureau, no grateful subsidiary's relationship to white philan-
thropists who might visit its campus as does Mr. Norton, the
northern capitalist, in *Invisible Man.* It did have a tie that I was
never quite able to fathom, because of what I had been conditioned to assume was the ironclad nature of America's commit-
ment to separation of church and state. That tie bound
Wilberforce, a church school, to the state of Ohio. Wilberforce's campus, when I was there, was bisected by a ravine.
Everything on one side of the ravine was called the "Church
Side" and was maintained by the AMEs. Everything on the
other side of the ravine was called the "State Side" and was
maintained by the state of Ohio. The "Church Side" now,
incidentally, is a separate institution, Wilberforce University.
The "State Side" now is an autonomous state college, Central
State University. But when I was going to college, both sides
had one president who happened then to be the holder of a
German doctorate and the son of the AME bishop whose position made him chairman of the university's board of trustees.
Once or twice while I was at Wilberforce I did see a committee
from the Ohio legislature on the campus. And I remember an
all-university convocation in honor of some legislators to
whom the bishop made a rousing plea for higher education
for the Negro which, despite the altruistic direct references
of its exalted rhetoric, even I could discern, was indirectly a
fervent plea for more state funds for Wilberforce. But whites
were not much in evidence at Wilberforce when I was there.
The "State Side" concentrated on teacher-training, trades, and
commercial subjects. It did seem to have more money and to
be better kept than the "Church Side." Yet the "Church Side,"
where I was, monopolized the liberal arts. It gave the prestige
degrees.

Both the "State Side" and the "Church Side" of my Wilberforce, however, were intensely Negro. Over all the campus,
ravine or no ravine, hovered the spirit of Daniel Alexander
Payne, the physically frail, indomitable AME bishop who had
founded the school. Behind Payne loomed the sacred appari-

tion of Richard Allen, founder of the African Methodist Episcopal Church and its first bishop, whom some have called the father of the American Negro. Negro history was inescapable at Wilberforce. The home of Colonel Charles Young, at that time the greatest military hero of the race, was just off the campus. Near the ravine was Homewood Cottage, where Hallie Q. Brown, at an advanced age, was still active. She had written *Homespun Heroines* and had gone to school with the children of physician-journalist Martin R. Delany, whose family had made its home at Wilberforce during Delany's later years. The Underground Railroad had run through Wilberforce. Tawawa Springs, a watering spot to which some of the more compassionate southern planters had once been wont to convey their favorite mulatto concubines and progeny, sloped down from the university infirmary. But what, perhaps, above all, made Wilberforce so intensely Negro, so proud and self-conscious of its past, was its belief that America in general tended to ignore places like Wilberforce. It was Wilberforce doctrine that most whites sanctioned only Negro enterprise in which whites could exercise the real hegemony.

One of the stories reflective of the atmosphere of Wilberforce when I was there has to do with Colonel Young. The colonel, a West Pointer, had not long been dead in 1925. He was a major when America entered World War I. He had hoped to be promoted and, as the first black American general, to lead combat troops in France. But army medical examiners had found fault with his health. Outraged, the major had mounted his horse at his Wilberforce home and ridden all the way to Washington. If he had hoped to prove his examiners a lie, he did not win. The army retired him as a colonel and sent him, instead of to France, to organize a constabulary for Liberia in Africa. It was gospel at Wilberforce that the army's exile of the colonel had hastened his death. (He died in Africa.) I am not sure but what it was not, according to the story, an African fever, or the *sequelae* of one, which immediately occasioned the colonel's demise. I have seen pictures of the colonel. Stern, erect, a rich dark brown, he looked out with a calm and steadfast eye upon a world he had been determined to have treat him as it treated any other man.

I did not go immediately from college into graduate school. My parents were concerned about my youth and inexperience, particularly since I had announced my intention to try for a master's degree at Columbia. I have always thought, however, that it was New York, and not Columbia, that gave my parents pause. I did not waste my year at home. I read voluminously. If I am sympathetic now when I hear undergraduates who are finishing college say that they would welcome a respite for a season from the lockstep of the academic processional, if I can believe that their motives are as often honorable as not, it may well be because I recall my own year of youthful leisure. So much that I had missed at college I made a part of me during that year. Then, just before I was scheduled to report to Columbia, my mother, the librarian at our Louisville high school, suddenly died. She had not been ill and she was a young woman. It was a tragedy for which my family was unprepared. My father, who had taught her and married her when she was only seventeen, I could see, in spite of his reserve, was deeply shaken. But he reminded me that life goes on. I remember how quiet he was, and yet how reassuring, when he and my brother escorted me to the train that bore me to New York.

That train bore me, also, into a new world. Yet, in at least one regard it merely extended the world I had always known. If in Louisville I had lived within a context of two worlds, one black and one white, and if the church and the white legislators at Wilberforce had repeated, as it were, for me, that same setting, with a split universe that was almost an exact duplication of the dichotomy of black and white that I had known in Louisville, in New York I entered another divided world. I spent my days at "white" Columbia and my nights in close communion with Negro Harlem. I lived again as I had always lived, within a veil. Inside the veil I moved without restraint.

Harlem was mine, all mine. Outside the veil I moved only as I had always moved, to use a phrase from the imagery of *Invisible Man,* in the enemy's country. I went to lectures at Columbia. I became familiar with the campus. I did use the library. It was, as a matter of fact, inside that huge and cavernous library, completely by myself, that I could be found for most of the many hours during which I essayed the role of a Columbia student. I never spoke to a professor. No professor ever spoke to me. The only Columbia student I established an acquaintance with was Melvin Tolson, with whom I shared a course in Victorian literature. I was no more a part of Columbia, except for its library, than I had been a part of the white folks' Louisville or of the white Ohio with which I had had a tenuous connection through the "State Side" at Wilberforce. I was, incidentally, not thereby distressed. To a young man, drunk as I was upon the promise and the hope of scholarship, being much alone with books and one's own thoughts can be something of a boon. My enforced solitude at Columbia was a boon to me. I could make my way from my lectures to the tranquil recesses of the library without interruption and without worrying over any distractions, once I had settled myself at a library desk. I did buy copies of the Columbia *Spectator,* the campus daily. I read it regularly. I knew very well who Nicholas Murray Butler was. I knew how eminent were some of my professors. I had one who had been decorated by a foreign government. Sometimes, privately and quietly, I prowled a little around Columbia. And sometimes, when I wanted a rest from reading, I would cross over Broadway and sit in a park from which I could gaze toward Grant's Tomb and the Riverside Church. I always walked to Columbia in the morning. I walked back to Harlem in the late afternoon or early evening.

Harlem of 1931 and early 1932, the Harlem that I first knew, was still the Harlem of the Harlem Renaissance, although the twenties were past and the Renaissance in its most storied days was over. Whether Harlem of the twenties was a prouder, livelier, more exciting, and more tonic place to be than my Harlem of the early thirties was, however, at least a debatable proposition. For Harlem in 1931 and 1932 was still the capital, not only of black America, but of Negroes everywhere. There was still, when I arrived there, nothing like Harlem elsewhere in the continental United States, or in the Caribbean, or in South America, or in Africa, or anywhere at all that Negroes could be found in numbers; and the Negroes who lived in Harlem knew that there was not. Moreover, Harlem in 1931 was not only a world capital for Negroes, it was also, for all Negroes everywhere, a mecca. On Seventh Avenue, Harlem's famous main thoroughfare, it was not unusual to hear then, as one of the virtually inevitable quips of the Harlem brand of those power brokers of conversation who make a business of saying what the crowd loves to hear, the playful admonition. "Stand here—just stand here long enough —and you'll see every Negro you ever knew."

I lived in Harlem at the "Y." Langston Hughes lived there, too, on the same floor with me. Cecil, the janitor on our floor, was a typical Harlemite. He was, that is, a migrant from the South. Indeed, Cecil was a Carolinian who had been bred to speak Gullah, the tongue, distinguished by its African survivals, which the black Sea Islanders, in their remoteness from the rest of America, have been able to preserve for three hundred years much as it was originally devised by them in their first adjustments to their once-new American environment. But neither Gullah nor the relative physical isolation of where the Gullahs live had prevented Cecil from hearing of Harlem or from making his way to it as to a promised land. Harlem of today may well be a place to which Cecil would not have come. When people speak of it, they tend to refer to dope and muggings, to vice and petty crime, to armies of jobless and welfare mothers easy with their sexual favors, and, above all, to horribly bad housing, to limited horizons of every kind, and to a hopeless slum. The Harlem that attracted Cecil was very different. Its reputation was not repellent. It attracted everybody, or, at least, every Negro—and not simply because of its cabarets, its Savoy Ballroom, its Cotton Club and Connie's Inn, its Lafayette Theater, its Renaissance Casino and Small's Paradise, its shows at the Apollo, and its night life at lesser well-known spots. I always thought of Cecil, for example, as a person who lived, if for any special avocation, for his religion (he worshipped in a Church of Fire Baptism). And had he told me that he had never heard of Florence Mills (most famous chorine of the Harlem Renaissance) or Claude McKay or that he had never been inside a Harlem club I would not have been inclined to doubt him. I knew why he had come to Harlem. He had not left the South seeking a good time. He had not come north to booze and gamble. He had come north because he was a "race" man. He was like Robert S. Abbott (affluent and powerful owner, publisher, and editor of the Chicago *Defender*), like the parents of Joe Louis, like "Pigfoot Mary" who would make a small fortune selling soul food on a Harlem street corner. He believed that, if only given the opportunity, the "race" would "progress." Moreover, he believed that it behooved a good "race" man to press for that opportunity. When I left him still in Harlem he had not abandoned his belief. Harlem had not yet begun to change enough to disillusion Cecil or to cease to be the capital and the mecca of the Negro world.

Seven months of Harlem and Columbia was all I was able to sustain, however, in 1931 and early 1932. The Great Depression drove me home to Louisville. I never returned to Columbia and never received a degree of any kind from there. It took me two years after my retreat from New York to get a job other than Works Progress Administration (WPA) employment.

But one day in 1932 a colored woman named Juliette Derricotte was injured in an automobile accident. She required emergency assistance and hospitalization; but the fact that she was female, the dean of women at Fisk, a cultivated person, and a figure of international importance in her profession made no difference in the vicinity of Dalton, Georgia, where she had the fatal misfortune to be. No hospital to which she could have been taken would receive her. She literally perished on the road, a victim of the incredible insanity of color caste. Fisk replaced her with an English teacher from one of the "colored" junior high schools in Louisville. And when, in 1934, that teacher finally decided not to return to Louisville, I replaced the English teacher.

So it was that at last I became permanently a teacher. The school to which I was summoned was then called Madison Junior High. It has since had a change of name. I stayed at Madison for eleven years. Then I went to Fisk University in Nashville for nine years. I followed my years at Fisk with fifteen years in Louisiana at Southern University. It was from Southern that I came to Chapel Hill.

If I have tended to remember Juliette Derricotte, if sometimes I reflect upon her tragic end, that is surely anything but strange. I knew her only through others. I never saw her and never exchanged words with her. I do have, in my mind's eye, what I believe is an excellent conception of how she looked. Her photograph was one of those which, at one time, appeared with some frequency in the Negro press. She was undoubtedly a mulatto, with hair and features that would hardly have embarrassed a debutante of debutantes in the purest circles of those "old families" which, in their halcyon days, reigned along Fifth Avenue and at Palm Beach and Newport. I do not know how dark she was. I suspect she could not have passed. On the other hand, I suspect that she seemed, even injured, what she undoubtedly was, a woman of very evident loveliness and refinement. How, then, could what did happen to her have happened? Were the people who obdurately refused her succor monsters? Were they prize hypocrites, for certainly they did their share of prating about their reverence for womanhood and the chivalry inherent in their southern way of life? Did they not often speak, both publicly and privately, in glowing encomia of the American character, with unmistakable innuendos that Americans were more humanitarian, as well

as more virtuous, than the residents of less benevolent and less
high-minded nations? I would have wagered that they did. But
I would also wager that they were, by and large, very ordinary
human beings, each having the usual self-contradictory com-
bination of strengths and weaknesses, and of good and bad
qualities, regularly to be discovered among all people everywhere. There may well have been a few genuine sadists among
them. There almost inevitably are in any fairly large selection
of randomly chosen representatives of our species. But it was
hardly sadism that accounted for Juliette Derricotte's death.
It was, in much greater likelihood, fear, fear of doing wrong
in the eyes of one's immediate neighbors. For the people who
let Juliette Derricotte die, like Juliette Derricotte, were the
victims of a system. The system told them what to do and what
not to do. To oppose the system meant, or could mean, trouble.
It could even mean big trouble—a job gone and no more
friends, a career blasted, even a whole life spent in limbo after
only one small lapse from grace. How to change the system
was not nearly so important to these people as their petty cares.
And, if their own petty cares probably obsessed them, so,
also, probably, did their own petty triumphs and gratifications.

A decade after Juliette Derricotte's death I was still teaching in Louisville and active in a liberal, decidedly biracial
organization then known as the Americans for Democratic
Action, or ADA. World War II was obviously drawing to its
close. ADA had concluded, I believe quite rightly, that it would
not be in the best interests of America, and particularly not in
the best interests of America's average man, to remove, as the
war ended, the wartime controls on such necessities as rent
and food. And so the Louisville chapter of ADA was organiz-
ing, with what it hoped was a great fanfare, and certainly
with the help of the major communication media of the area
(most of whose important figures belonged to ADA), a mass
meeting of Louisville citizens. The idea was that the mass meeting would demonstrate the mounting volume of popular sentiment against the abandonment of controls and that the political

potential of this demonstration could then be transmitted with undiminished effect to Washington. Louisville had a municipal auditorium. To house the mass meeting the ADA had secured the auditorium. About a week before the scheduled mass meeting, a Negro college sorority gave a program there which it sponsored annually. Every seat in the auditorium was occupied. It was one of those programs in which many participants get to be seen. Costumes were worn. There was much singing and dancing, and not a little declaiming of noble views. Prizes were given, too, for the program was constructed around the rivalry between competing groups, all of which were obliged to exercise their ingenuity in the exemplification of a common theme. The exact wording of the theme on this occasion, I do not recollect. It had to do, however, with the building of a New Jerusalem in postwar America—indeed, in all of the postwar world. Thus, it was that for three hours, if not longer, a capacity audience, almost exclusively Negro, applauded to the rafters the gleaming vistas of the future presented for its delectation in the municipal auditorium. I particularly recall how gleaming vista after gleaming vista that the audience approved suggested, through that approval, a readiness, and probably a messianic zeal, on the part of the enthusiastic viewers, to lend a hand and put their shoulders to the wheel in working for a brave new world.

It was only a few days later, in the same auditorium, that the ADA held its highly publicized mass meeting, with almost every seat unoccupied.

I have already spoken of the fun I had as I grew up in Louisville. I had fun, too, as I taught in Louisville. My days at school were full. Junior-high-school teachers have no vacant time. I met twenty-five classes a week every week. I consulted with my homeroom class at least twice each day. I performed "extra duties" at recess. I kept records. They multiplied as the years went by. I found, too, that a junior-high-school teacher cannot escape involvement with the community outside his school. My

Columbia professors could emerge, remote as the farther stars, from undisclosed retreats, volley their erudition at their classes from behind invisible barriers, and retire unperturbed into the dim privacies whence they came without really even seeing who their students were. At Madison Junior High School teachers were literally, as well as legally, *in loco parentis*. There was no restraining wall between them and the students they confronted. Once I did feebly interpose an objection to my principal when I and my fellow teachers were instructed to peer down our homeroom students' throats for symptoms of diphtheria. I would not have known what I was looking for, and, moreover, I had the disquieting notion that diphtheria was possibly contagious. Even so, to be *in loco parentis* to one's students sometimes took one into students' homes to talk with their actual parents. It meant that everywhere one went in Louisville one was on display, for everywhere in Louisville one's students might, and usually did, turn up. *In loco parentis!* The phrase has stuck with me through all these years. It added new dimensions of both intensity and ubiquity to my contacts with my own hometown. If closet scholarship had ever been conceivable for me, my Louisville teaching forever ended any such eventuality. The sense of being an extension of every student's ego that my Louisville teaching bred into me, as well as the feeling it left implanted deep within me of the impact upon my students' classroom situations of vectors of influence originating often far, far from those classrooms in acts and critical decisions of which my students and I might well not be aware, helped to account for activities of mine not assigned to me by my superiors and not always the kind of expenditure of talents that a teacher's range of duties requires.

Some of those activities, it is true, did bear closely upon my teaching. Louisville, when I started teaching there, as was standard practice throughout the South, penalized its Negro teachers for being Negro by imposing upon them a pay differential. Every Negro teacher in Louisville made 15 percent less in salary than any white teacher of identical training and experience. During my years of teaching in Louisville we Negro teachers erased that differential. I worked with the group that led the fight against the differential. It was in the early days of the National Association for the Advancement of Colored People's legal strategy against color discrimination. We got aid and counsel from the national office of the NAACP. But we got aid and counsel, too, from whites who lived in Louisville. Our entente with the NAACP lifted us above one kind of parochialism. Through it we acquired an intimate sense of a big picture, of social stresses and attempts at their redress, which extended upon occasion throughout an entire nation. We saw, too, how our own local problems often fit into this bigger picture. Our entente with our local whites lifted us above the parochialism of black separatism. The nucleus of our white supporters were people connected with the *Courier-Journal,* the Louisville *Times,* and the radio station WHAS, three enterprises owned largely, if not completely, by the Bingham family. Barry Bingham, the son of the head of the family, was part of the white nucleus. So was Wilson Wyatt, who became mayor of Louisville before I left the town.

After we eliminated the salary differential we joined with the whites who had supported us in other efforts aimed at improving Louisville. Some of those efforts attacked ways of demeaning Negroes. Others attacked injustices we all wanted to ameliorate in which race was not an issue. In the summers I went to school, though not at Columbia. I have already indicated that, after I once quit Columbia, I never returned. Now I chose the University of Michigan. I took my master's there in four summers and continued, motoring up to Ann Arbor every June, to work on what might at some future date become my Ph.D.

However, something about my life at this stage that must be said I have not yet said. A goodly portion of it had nothing to do with any cause. It was play, with no end that I could describe other than expressing my own vitality. Earlier I called the Negro Louisville of my youth the truest democracy I have ever known. Perhaps a correlative of size is represented in this judgment. The population of my Negro Louisville never exceeded fifty thousand persons. It was thus large enough for us who were part of it not to be plagued with village viruses. On the other hand it was not so large that our local magnates and celebrities were synthesized images rather than accessible mortals like ourselves whom we could strip bear of any layers of pretense, since people in our community were constantly exposed to close scrutiny, if not by everyone of us at least always by someone whom we knew. Nor was our Louisville so large that it was riven with class barriers. One of the biggest weddings of my time in Negro Louisville, in a high Episcopalian service, united a woman teacher and sorority girl with a chauffeur.

Of the two unself-consciously egalitarian poolrooms on Walnut Street, Negro Louisville's Broadway, at which I shot pool, without a thought of loss of status, the noisier one secreted a huge round table in a back room for patrons whose sporting instincts yearned, not for pool, but for games of chance. Incidentally, in this particular poolroom, as was to be expected, I shot against any adversary who was available. One of my more frequent adversaries, however, came to be a pimp, a man much older than I, a gentle soul with a pockmarked face and the general demeanor of a graying Casper Milquetoast. He and I punctuated our runs of balls, not only with good-natured derision of each other's skill, but also with elaborate discussions of current events, for this adversary of mine read at least five or six newspapers daily. Pimps today, as everybody knows, thrive on vice and violence. They beat their women and feed them dope and drive big flashy cars. This Louisville pimp of a bygone era would have abhorred violence of any kind, and the ostentation of some of his successors would have appalled and perplexed him mightily. He still thought that his profession was one of those that a discreet regard for the opinions of mankind abjured him to dissemble. He lived in a *ménage à trois* in a tidy, two-story, red-brick edifice. The residents of the first floor may have been, for all

I know, as hidebound in their morality as Mrs. Grundy. My pimp and the two women who supported him were tenants of the second floor. The women were young. I sometimes saw them on the street, where they would hardly have seemed out of character attended by small children of their own.

Not too far from their domicile was the Phyllis [*sic*] Wheatley Branch of the YWCA, another tidy, red-brick edifice. In the YWCA, on one Sunday of each month, met a forum. Who sponsored the forum I forget. But it attracted steadily an audience that filled the room provided for it. I attended many of the forums. For much of my enjoyment of Negro Louisville was in its talk. Many nights for me ended at a tavern called Dave's Bar, after my more serious pursuits were done. At Dave's the hum of voices never died. Most of the talk, of course, was persiflage. But some of it did touch on grave concerns. And once, at Dave's, I observed a silence that was memorable. It was during World War II. A boyish-looking lieutenant and the pretty girl who sensuously clung to him had been an epicenter of drinking and witticisms at the bar when another lieutenant entered Dave's and summoned the first lieutenant into an empty booth. There was, I saw, a reception of a letter in the booth, by the first lieutenant. I should add that the days had come during World War II when America had finally entered Europe, through the Italian boot. Along rugged terrain from Naples to Rome, American fighting men were being killed. What the second lieutenant had delivered to the first were orders, orders that would send the first lieutenant to "replace" one of those men who had been killed. As the first lieutenant paid the bartender's score, I could not fail to note, he had ceased to effervesce. His tongue was mute.

When I went to Fisk, World War II was over, but many American males of college and university age were still overseas or in uniform within the states. In my first semesters at Fisk the student body was predominantly female. Soon the men were back, but even with them Fisk was not, in numbers, a large school. I think its greatest enrollment, while I was on its faculty, did not quite reach a thousand. Even so, with the possible exception of Howard, a school nine or ten times its size, Fisk was as cosmopolitan as any Negro school anywhere. In the early 1950s the Fisk campus newspaper analyzed the provenience of Fisk's student body. The paper found that the Fisk student emanated from over forty states (there are—or were, in the 1950s—states in America of which it could almost be said that no Negroes lived in them) and several foreign countries. I could not equate my experience at Fisk with my experience in Louisville. I was never, for instance, to be a part of Nashville as I had been a part of Negro Louisville. I was never again to be so malleable, and so amenable to sympathetic communion with my environment, as I had been in Louisville. College teaching was not like teaching in a junior high school. I think I came to know some of my students at Fisk very well, perhaps even better than I knew any of my students in Louisville, but I never stood in the same relation to them as I had stood in relation to my junior-high-school charges. And then, Fisk itself was not Louisville. Fisk itself was another, and a rather unique, universe.

Fisk was founded in 1866. One of the discarded army barracks in which it first held classes is still on its campus. In the 1870s cash and other contributions vital to its survival were raised in the tours on two continents of its famed Jubilee Singers. It is difficult to speak of the Jubilee Singers without being emotionally affected. They conquered wherever they went. Usually they sang before charmed hosts of listeners. Sometimes they sang in camera for the great. Queen Victoria heard them. So did Kaiser Wilhelm I. The songs that made them famous were the Negro spirituals: "Swing Low, Sweet Chariot"; "I Couldn't Hear Nobody Pray?"; "Go Down Moses"; "Deep River." DuBois, a Fisk alumnus, would call such songs the "Sorrow Songs." And Fisk has not forgotten, nor has it repudiated, these sorrow songs or those who sang them. A mammoth painting of the original Jubilee Singers, surrogates for the slaves, hangs, quaint dress and all, in a place of honor in the Fisk Chapel, dominating the choir loft. Jubilee Hall and the Oval before it command the campus. No Fisk president has dared to do anything with Jubilee Hall except renovate and remodel it, always carefully retaining its distinctive basic features. For many years each Fisk president lived in a home called Heritage House. It cannot be said that Fisk has rejected its past or that it has averted its eyes from the circumstance that its first students were former slaves. Its social scientists and its humanists in literature, art, and music have emphasized inquiry into the black experience. Its library has followed suit, with collections about the Negro which are known and respected by all who are acquainted with the study of the Negro. Intellectually, Fisk has done its part to foster racial solidarity, to remind all Negroes of their common roots. Socially, however, Fisk is a center of Negro Belgravia. The Negro middle class sends its children to Fisk. Children of other Negroes avid for social mobility are also among those who seek the imprimatur of the Fisk degree. Across a street from Fisk is Meharry Medical College, where over half of America's Negro doctors have been trained. Fisk coeds expect to marry Meharry doctors, and often do. The rather unique distinction of Fisk is its blend of race and class. It champions the lowly and preserves its own folk origins while its well-groomed faculty, when I was there, sipped tea, served by maids, on Wednesday afternoons in Heritage House.

It was while I was at Fisk that I began the first of the essays that constitute this book. I did not have a doctorate when I went to Fisk, though I had done some work beyond the master's. I was not passionately devoted to Negro literature. Indeed, I thought of it as I thought of all literature. I had always read it. I may hardly have been in the second grade when I first publicly recited Paul Laurence Dunbar's "Ode to Ethiopia," and, during the 1920s, the years of the Harlem Renaissance, I read the poetry and fiction of the Renaissance as it first appeared. I attribute to the New Critics, or at least to an oblique impetus I received from them, the fact that I became particularly, and

partisanly, interested in the Negro writer. At Fisk, understandably, I accelerated my attempts to earn a doctorate. And
so at Ann Arbor I was reading the New Critics. But at Fisk also,
in our general literature course for sophomores, the last
English requirement of Fisk's general-education core for all of
its undergraduates, the textbook in use was *Approach to Literature,* two of the editors of which were Cleanth Brooks and
Robert Penn Warren. I encountered New Critical theory and
practice, therefore, whether I was at home, as it were, at Fisk,
or abroad, in Ann Arbor. Moreover, if the New Critics were
inhospitable to the Romantic movement, I thought I could
easily extrapolate from their disdain for the Romantics a
probably even greater disdain for the writers of my race. Indeed, my suspicions were, if admittedly only based on inference, somewhat corroborated, it seemed to me, in a remark
made to me by a professor at Michigan—a professor whom I
esteemed, not only because of his eminence in his area of
specialization, but also because of his many kindnesses to me.
This professor and I were speaking about irony. One hardly
spoke of anything else in those days, unless it was ambiguity. I
was thinking of a subject for a doctoral dissertation and had
mentioned the possibility of a study of irony in Negro fiction.
This professor, and my friend, who was certainly no bigot, but
who almost surely wanted to warn me of a possible lion in my
path which it might be well for me not to ignore, reminded me
of the then-prevailing tendency to see irony as a subtle thing,
too subtle, especially in the judgment of some converts to New
Criticism, for the limited competence of most, if not all, Negro
writers.

I did write a doctoral dissertation on irony in Negro fiction.
Actually, the issue of how competent Negro writers were to
handle subtlety seemed moot to me insofar as the irony in
Negro fiction was concerned. All Negro fiction, as I saw it,
tended to protest, and to protest a single irony, the irony of the
way Negroes were mistreated in a country that espoused democracy as democracy was espoused in America. My position

was simple. Irony might be ever so subtle, but all ironies were not. Of those which were not, among the least subtle was the irony of American racism. I was hard put, after years of meeting Negroes from every walk of life, to recall a solitary one who did not view his own gratuitous misadventures solely because of his color as an outcome incongruous to what he should have expected according to the American creed. And so I did not question the presence of irony in Negro fiction. All that seemed debatable to me was the quality of the irony, and the quality of the irony led me, I theorized, where it should lead in a doctoral dissertation of a critical nature, into a discussion of art—in my case, of the art in, or not in, Negro fiction.

Within less than two years of the day on which I completed my doctorate at Ann Arbor I departed Fisk. I went to Louisiana. The Deep South was relatively new to me. Southern University was a different world from the bourgeois enclave at Fisk. I had not been at Southern long when a teacher took me to her home only an hour's ride from the Southern campus. The teacher was chic in fashion's latest mode. We rode in her car, a model of the year then current. She had been, her father confided to me proudly after dinner, even while she was in college, the fastest and the best cotton picker in the parish. From the bridge that spans the Mississippi River at Baton Rouge I could see westward toward tilled fields, but, for miles downriver, I looked toward the metal and masonry of great industrial plants. In the river there would almost surely always be ocean-going vessels, come from foreign lands, with bauxite for Kaiser's Aluminum or crude oil for the Esso refinery. The girl and the panorama from the bridge signified for me the presence of cultural change which I found at Southern. Over 90 percent, perhaps over 95 percent, of Southern's students were born and reared in Louisiana. Some of them were city-bred, from New Orleans or Baton Rouge or Shreveport. But many of them were the children of parents who still belonged to the agrarian economy of cotton and sugar cane cultivation.

There were French names at Southern, too, and sometimes
Cajun speech slipped off a student's tongue. At Fisk the shadow
of the plantation lingered only as in a museum. At Southern
the Negro's folk past and present were visible and animate
in the background of many of its students. As the president of
Southern was wont to say, at times perhaps too unctuously,
Southern, a land-grant institution, was a people's college. And
its people were not, like those of Fisk, the black bourgeoisie.
Its people were those about whom Leadbelly chanted. They
were farm laborers and an urban proletariat whose sons and
daughters now were going to college. If I had ever wanted to
see two worlds meet, I saw them meet at Southern. The old
plantation-centered South met the industrial North, which
was North no more, but the current American dream. For the
Old South was passing. Its social customs were yielding, however stubbornly, to an America in which the airport at Minne-
apolis was only different in nonessentials from the airport at
New Orleans.

I perhaps saw less of students at Southern than I had seen
of them either in Louisville or at Fisk. At Southern I was first a
department head and, then, the graduate dean. Yet I think I
did come to know the Southern student fairly well. I think I
came, also, to have some sense of his world. The criticism I had
begun to write at Fisk I continued to write at Southern. The
books I had wanted to write, I told myself now, I did not write
because of the extent to which my time and energies were
preempted by administrative duties. That may have been true.
It may have been only a plausible alibi. But it led me also into a
chain of alibis, not only for myself, but for Negro would-be
productive scholars as a general class, all of whom, it seemed to
me, taught too many courses or had been seduced into administration. I had become increasingly familiar with my Negro
colleagues in English scholarship. They, in substantially every
case, taught at Negro schools and, after all, there were only, in
round numbers, about a hundred Negro institutions of higher
learning in the entire nation. Moreover, I was active in the Col-

lege Language Association (CLA), the organization of teachers of language and literature in Negro schools. I was even, at a point in the 1950s, its president. And so I knew the Negroes who were writing criticism. I knew, too, what I thought were their peculiar problems. Indeed, most of those problems I thought I shared. They began with a set of what I supposed could be called traditional assumptions. Briefly and badly stated, those assumptions postulated that Negroes had written neither very much nor very well. Moreover, they had written mostly about Negroes who, when I was younger, were hardly deemed of sufficient importance to constitute a subject for significant writing. In the busy, highly competitive world of productive scholarship, merely to adopt Negro literature as a specialty, therefore, was to adopt a pariah. I always thought, incidentally, that more, or less, than simple racism was involved in the proscriptions on Negro literature. I was old enough, for instance, to remember when American literature was something of an interloper in the empire of literary study, when Sydney Smith's "Who Reads an American Book, or Sees an American Play?" was still, more than a century after its delivery, and on *this* side of the Atlantic, all too reliable an index of the superciliousness with which the palace guard in the academic establishment maintained a quasicolonial attitude toward American literature. It must be conceded, of course, that Negro literature was, when I began writing about it, still relatively sparse. As late as the end of the 1940s, a diligent graduate student who could concentrate on his task might well have been able to read every Negro novel extant within a summer (he would need to be, incidentally, a real prodigy at speed reading to do so now). But, even so, I felt that Negro literature, by the time I wrote my doctoral dissertation, had acquired both sufficiently distinctive form and adequately extensive content to justify its serious consideration as an object of study by respectable scholars. I never did feel that these respectable scholars could only, or should only, be black. Yet I was not happy at a tendency I thought I detected on the part of some white scholars

to acquiesce all too complacently in the game of racial stereotypes when they analyzed Negro writing. No matter, therefore,
how much I respected the pains a white scholar like Vernon
Loggins had taken in assembling data for his *The Negro Author
in America: His Development in America to 1900*, or how appreciative I was that he should have ventured off the beaten path to
work with Negro literature, I was, nevertheless, disturbed when
he spoke of Jupiter Hammon's "mystic Negro mind" and of the
"instinct for music which is so strong in his [*i.e.,* Hammon's]
race," or when Lorenzo Blackson, who was born in Delaware
and whose parents also were of American birth, in *The Rise and
Progress of the Kingdoms of Light and Darkness*, written in the
1860s, appeared to Loggins to have composed, in this book, a
"product of . . . a pure African temperament." If I asked myself how Blackson, without ever spending any time in Africa
or having any intimate contact with Africans had acquired this
"pure African temperament" I could only answer: through
some mysterious agency of transmission, perhaps through the
"blood" passed on to him by his parents from African forebears. I could only account for Jupiter Hammon's "racial"
instincts by reasoning that seemed to me equally absurd. And I
did detect, if not an absurdity, at least as great an addiction to
mythological pronouncements about "the Negro," in some of
Robert Bone's later determinations of what was, and what was
not, verisimilitude in the depiction of Negro life. From my own
predilections, then, I could argue that I, and my contemporary
Negro colleagues in the criticism of Negro literature, did represent a point of view that should be heard by students of
American life. We held that, just as it was helpful, if not truly
necessary, in reading other American writers to possess an
organized and critical knowledge of American life and letters,
so, too, in reading Negro writers, and reading them at a proper
level of informed recognition and appreciative comprehension,
one should be possessed of an organized and critical knowledge
of Negro life and letters. Our position did array us against
everyone who dismissed Negro writers as relatively isolated

phenomena occurring like sports in nature, or who thought of the total corpus of Negro writing as too inconsequential to be a literature, if not also too lacking in those elements of cohesion and scope that are imperative in a genuine literature. From the premises we shared we were, as we saw it, often on the defensive. We were, perhaps, especially defensive on issues of aesthetics. Much Negro writing, we admitted, was crude and clumsy; but enough of it, we also thought, was truly art to warrant further our contention that there was a Negro literature. We were undoubtedly informed at least a little by a sense of mission and by a conviction that our lot, in our engagement with Negro literature, was that of crusaders. And, if we thought of ourselves as voices crying in a wilderness, that was perhaps understandable. We controlled only the *CLA Journal* and could be called a part of an inner circle only at *Phylon*, the *Journal of Negro History*, the *Journal of Negro Education*, and in a scattering of additional periodicals edited by Negroes, some of which were not so stable as those already named. We controlled no presses, no publishing houses, and no foundations or endowments that subsidized scholarly activity.

We who were in this band of older Negro critics do not feel today as we felt in the years I have just described. We still have grievances and still think that too much of our program has not been adopted. But change has ensued. At Fisk a quarter of a century ago I sat in a group that was talking with Nevil Shute, the English novelist. He had just been to India, which was then in the throes of establishing itself as an independent member of the British Commonwealth. His mind was on change, on welcoming and helping change. Indeed, he had come to Fisk to suggest that some of the young people on our campus entertain the prospect of a life in India. It was his notion that, during its transition from an old subserviency to a new autonomy, India would need Western expertise. He reasoned that India might be readier to accept such expertise from American Negroes than from white Britishers or whites of any kind. I can hear him now, and reconstitute the scene around him, as if it all were only yesterday. Within a large, handsomely appointed room called the International Student Center we spoke with each other in temperate, conversational tones. Outside, a Tennessee evening graduated from dusk into night. At an appointed moment a carillon struck chimes.

I did not then, I do not now, despise Shute and his mission. His visit to Fisk was at his own expense. He was moved by a sincere desire, as he could envision the future, to do, within the limits imposed by circumstance on him, what he could to make that future better than the past. What impresses me now, however, is how little he saw of what that actual future would turn out to be. Yet I do not think that a Nevil Shute, or anyone, looking into the future before our time would have missed what was actually to happen as much as everyone in the last thirty years has failed to foresee the present. For our present world is, as rarely or never before, a world of change. What would have happened to any of our Fisk undergraduates or junior faculty had they gone to India, I cannot surmise. What has happened to them in America has been epochal.

Yet it has not merely happened to them. They, and others even younger than they, have helped it happen. Civil-rights activism in their own country probably overshadows for them any other thing that could have, or has, happened in India or elsewhere, even in Africa or Vietnam. And the changes wrought by this civil-rights activism have certainly had far-reaching effects in America. Such changes are not the only source of change in the treatment of Negro literature. But they are important. Added to them are the rather explosive growth of the literature itself, the increase in Negro literacy, the urbanization of the American Negro, the peculiar temperament of the twentieth century, with its secularization, its science and scientism, and its cult of innovation, and the continuing evolutionary processes in American life, which reflect the dynamic, rather than static, nature of the American mentality and of American society as a whole.

And so it is that the essays in this collection may well be

social documents as well as individual expressions. They do represent activity that began years ago. With this introductory essay I have sought to provide a frame of reference which might illuminate that activity. I am, for example, an integrationist. That I am, I believe, evidences itself in my approach to literature. Surely, I have intellectual arguments to support my integrationism. But beyond those, and certainly as a powerful factor in everything I have tried to write, is my experience of life. Thus it may well be that, when I read an invocation of black separatism, an important mainspring of my reaction is cultural—a consequence, that is to say, of my youth in Louisville and at Wilberforce and Columbia, and of my affinities for the present older generation of Negro scholars. I could not justify this introductory essay if I did not firmly believe that what I have just said is true. On the other hand, it is only one aspect of truth. There are thoughts and feelings that we have and things that we do which we do not wish to attribute to any pressures upon us merely of environment. We like to think that some of our judgments are based upon uses of our faculties that transcend moments and milieus. We like to think that, sometimes, we are right in an eternal sense. I would like to think that some things in these essays which follow are right in that eternal sense and that their utility, therefore, does not cease with their revocation of a recent past but extends also into their implications for a present that should always be, the present that the sincere humanist thinks of when he thinks of what would be for him a decent and a valid world.

An Essay
in
Criticism

I BEGAN *writing about Negro literature early in the 1940s. The exact circumstances of my beginning, as I remember them now, tell something, in their way, about Negro life.*

There are four Negro college fraternities. The oldest of the four, for obvious reasons, is named Alpha Phi Alpha. It is, incidentally, called Alpha, and its members are known as either "Alphas" or "Apes." But the circumstance about the Alphas which tells something about Negro life (and which would be true about any Negro college fraternity, sororities included) is that the Alphas could not be simply a college fraternity. They had to be a social-action group, doing their bit for the advancement of the race.

Alpha men were, and many still are (even in the changed 1970s), Alpha men for life. The fraternity's so-called graduate chapters out-number its undergraduate chapters. For years the fraternity vigorously prosecuted its famous (among Negroes) "Go to High School, Go to College" campaign. Its general presidents have tended to be quite eminent men in the national Negro community—men like Charles H. Wesley and Rayford Logan, the historians and champions of Negro rights, or Belford Lawson, a lawyer active in the cause of civil rights, or Frank Stanley, publisher of the Louisville **Defender***, who, as president of the national organization of Negro newspaper owners, publishers, and editors, in the 1940s and 1950s played a prominent role in fighting racial discrimination of several kinds, especially in the armed services.*

General presidents of Alpha campaigned for their office almost as if they were running for a high post in the national government. It was incumbent upon them to shout from the housetops their achievements as "race" men. They said very little, though always something, about the "social" side of college life. In view of the conduct of these Alpha general presidents and all aspirants to the Alpha general presidency, as well as the sense of mission that permeated all Alphadom (and, indeed, all of Negro Greekdom), no one should be surprised to learn that The Sphinx, *the official journal of the Alphas, had its sense of mission too. It could not be content merely with circulating amiable gossip about Alphas among the Alpha brotherhood.*

My career, then, as a critic of Negro literature, as I remember it, really started when I became the books editor of The Sphinx. *It would have been impossible for me, in the early 1940s, to have been that kind of editor in a magazine like* The Sphinx *without talking about Negro literature.*

"An Essay in Criticism" appeared in Phylon *in the last quarter of 1950.* Phylon *was a quarterly founded by W. E. B. DuBois (who happened to be an Alpha) when he went back to the changed Atlanta University after his feud with Walter White—a gentleman who could be, upon occasion, as intractable as DuBois (and who also happened to be an Alpha)—reached unmanageable proportions. Primarily a learned journal for social scientists,* Phylon *was, nevertheless, in 1950, the leading resource for publication about Negro literature under the control of Negroes.*

DuBois was no longer associated with Atlanta University in 1950. A sociologist of some distinction, Mozell Hill, was editing Phylon. *Under Hill's direction,* Phylon *celebrated the middle year of the twentieth century with a symposium about the American Negro that filled all the pages of a special issue. Contributions for this special issue were solicited. In fact, all of the articles in the special issue were by invitation only. Writers who appeared in this issue included Arna Bontemps, Gwendolyn Brooks, Sterling Brown, G. Lewis Chandler, Nick Aaron Ford, Hugh M. Gloster, Robert Hayden, Langston Hughes, Ulysses Lee, Alain Locke, Charles H. Nichols, L. D. Reddick, Saunders Redding, Ira De A. Reid, George S. Schuyler, William Gardner Smith, Era Bell Thompson, and Margaret Walker.*

What I had written about Negro literature in The Sphinx *and one or two other places had apparently caught the eye of Mozell Hill and his fellow editors at* Phylon. *I was very proud on my invitation to appear in this special midcentury issue of* Phylon. *I was also very conscious of art as art. I was working on a doctoral dissertation on irony. And so, when one considers the Alphas and my invitation to be in* Phylon *and the nature of my dissertation, perhaps that I should choose to try to speak as I tried to speak in "An Essay in Criticism" was inevitable.*

⋈

I think it is a truism that in every regard the Negro writer has been typically American, except, perhaps, in the amount and quality of his work. Whether in absolute or comparative terms, the Negro has not published much in America. Likewise, whether in absolute or comparative terms, his writing has been too often execrable, although throughout the course of Negro literature constant improvement is readily discernible.

Now the problems of both the quantity and the quality of Negro literature are, it seems to me, inextricably intertwined with the problem of the Negro writer's audience. It is nonsense to say that a writer's audience does not influence him, just as nonsensical as it is to hold that writers write — and permit themselves to be published — merely because there is something in them that must come out. And the Negro writer has lacked a helpful audience in two large ways: *viz.*, sympathetically and critically. The lack of a wide sympathetic audience among the only extensive public available to him has undoubtedly inhibited the Negro writer's effective use of symbols; and, of course, creative writing is nothing if not symbolic. However, eliminating the iniquities of racial stereotypes, the indispensable propaedeutic for easing the Negro writer's problem in the handling of symbols, must continue to wait upon the combined action of many forces — among them, incidentally, the services of a competent and forthright critical audience. On the other hand the lack of critical audience is clearly a reflection on Negro literary scholarship more than on anything else.

For Negroes just have not gotten around to real criticism of their own literature. We have done some good things. But all our accomplishments can quickly be demonstrated to be mere prolegomena for the hard, serious, tedious labor of giving our literature the sort of scholarly and critical framework that adds the needed marginal dimensions to the established European literatures. Let us look at the best we have done in criticism. Saunders Redding's *To Make a Poet Black* is a rapid summary, mainly historical, moving too hastily to develop adequately his thesis that Negro literature is a literature of necessity, though often enough delighting us with such trenchant *obiter dicta* as its characterization of Joel Chandler Harris' dialect. Hugh Gloster's more recent *Negro Voices in American Fiction* is an excellent reference work, with an especially valuable bibliography; but, again, Gloster is limited by intentions that are as patently summary as Redding's. Sterling Brown, who has done yeoman work in the area of his choice, has found himself completely occupied with the job of getting Negro literature into the field of vision of a wide public. Benjamin Brawley was always as timid and platitudinous as a Sunday School pamphlet. James Weldon Johnson was an executive, and his criticism, while often redeemed by his native taste, betrayed that tendency of his disposition as well as his lack of academic scholarship. There is little more to say about Negroes' criticism of their own literature, except that here for Negro students with ability and industry is a veritable green pasture.

Sometimes I have dreamed dreams about what could transpire in the criticism of Negro literature. Dreams can be very magnificent. DuBois, half a century ago at Atlanta, bursting with the enthusiasm of his youth, laid down, it will be remembered, a program for an integrated sociological study of the Negro problem that was to have carried through a hundred years. Incidentally, during the thirteen years that he then stayed at Atlanta, he maintained his program's operation largely according to plan. And I have wished that those of us working with Negro literature might catch some of the magnificence—foolish, arrogant, but, withal, glorious—of young DuBois'

Atlanta dreaming. I do not begrudge a single one of the buildings I see going up on Negro campuses. God knows when one wanders around the great university campuses of America and then comes South again, he knows all too bitterly how much, in the "segregated but equal" dispensation, we are still on short rations. And if one moves through the parts of Negro ghettos where most Negroes have to live, perceiving unavoidably the squalor and meanness everywhere, scrofulous hovels jammed together, filthy, unkept streets, bad odors and harsh atmospheres, he will give thanks for every bit of clean turf, every piece of modern plumbing, every gracious contour on the Negro college campus. It is, indeed, always a matter of great wonder to me, when I recall where Negroes have been cooped up, that we are not all snarling, venomous beasts. After all, how can any man esteem beauty who knows nothing of it? Let us, then, get what we can of beauty on our physical campuses.

And yet—I would sometimes that our college budgets did occasionally contemplate a series of studies in our literature. I can at least pretend names for them: the Atlanta University Series of American Negro Writers; the James T. Shephard Editions of Slave Narratives; the Tennessee State College Studies in Negro Literary Acculturation. I can think, too, of individual studies prepared, if not issued also, under the aegis of some Negro school that has somehow or other managed to institute a program of research. This business of dialect—we have now reached a state of cultural assurance sufficient for us to put it in its right perspectives, both linguistically and psychologically—I should like to see studied. What we know, or ought to know, about the fictional treatment of the Negro middle class has never been systematically assembled. There are handbooks and anthologies of Negro poetry, but no single intensive studies of separate poems of any Negro poets. And, of course, the possibilities for tracing the relations of Negro literature are, as one would expect, virtually legion. Because Negroes have not written in great volume, or because some people say that Negro art is shallow, a dream like this may seem far-fetched. It is not. One competent and diligent student, Lorenzo Dow Turner, working — one almost wants to say bare-handed — in the field of linguistics has shown how rich can be the yield from sources that might appear barren to the superficial eye. Moreover, some of the things I suggest have already been attempted. I know, although I have seen neither of them, that within the last several years at least two problems in research have dealt with the too-long-neglected slave narratives. Some time ago Brawley did for Chapel Hill a life of Paul Laurence Dunbar, the first of a series, never continued, which William Edward Farrison tells me Brawley was to have edited. It is a shockingly inadequate and old-maidish performance, but still it was a start. Certainly the materials to justify a host of enterprises by students of Negro literature do exist. The problem is in getting people who know what to do with these materials, and who, moreover, are prepared to endure the drudgery that sustained scholarship demands.

Indeed our literature is thin, not altogether because of its own inherent limitations, but because we have not enriched it and expanded it with the great accretions of interpretation we are likely to recall every time we read a fairly familiar piece of literature by a white author reputable enough to be in the literary histories. To realize this one need not go to Shakespeare, around whom the critical works are so numerous that they literally do constitute fair-sized libraries. One may select almost at random comparatively minor figures in the kingdom of English letters and still have quite a bit of bibliographical sport with them. But, in terms of the assistance that a good critical audience can provide, Negro literature is starved.

Waiving for the moment the possible contributions of diligent research, consider merely the province of aesthetic judgments. There are so many issues to be noted and discussed and argued about in that area alone that we have not set down as fully as we might. There is, for instance, in *One Way to Heaven* the way that Countee Cullen wrote two novels; the larger one about two "little" people, for all that it simpers occasionally, has much of the charm of a fairy story, but the other — which is not fitted too well into the whole — while worthy of commendation as an attempt healthily to laugh at one's self, is too stilted and self-conscious for good satire. Or, since we have started with *One Way to Heaven,* there is also the trouble generally that Negro writers have in writing good, convincing conversation, a trouble especially distressing in comedy-of-manners work like the satirical episodes in Cullen's novel where he brings people together for drawing-room talk, but gets out of them only a painful burlesque of the brilliant stream of *mots* on which one floats gaily through the ether of William Congreve or Oscar Wilde or George Bernard Shaw. And there are countless other items, each of them conceivably a "rift to be loaded with ore": like the way in which — for all the nobility of her intentions, because she is herself so naively philistine, so breathless with adoration of good-looking people Nordic style (even when they are tinted with the tar brush), good-looking clothes, good-looking homes, and country-club ideas of the *summa bona* — Jessie Fauset's defenses of the Negro middle class backfire into an indictment of her horrid copycatting of the wrong values. Or, to speak again of conversation, consider the verisimilitude (as ordinary Negro speech) of the talk in Zora Neale Hurston's *Moses, Man of the Mountain* and the superb rightness of this assimilation of the Old Testament story to Negro mores when Miss Hurston's retelling of the famous Hebrew legend is diagramed, as it should be, allegorically, so that other beautiful hits — like the equation of Moses, from the house of Pharaoh, to our mulatto leadership, or of the grumbling of the Hebrews in the wilderness to the attitudes that Negro masses take toward Negro leaders — assume their due proportions in this parable about one minority group intimated through the tale of another. Or, for perhaps even better art, reflect upon the life-giving quality of Ann Petry's imagination in *The Street,* an achievement the magnitude of which can be sharply realized by placing beside Miss Petry's Lutie Johnson — a woman warm and vital, whose senses, and will, pulse with a fierce indwelling energy—the stillborn and crudely manipulated Mimi Daquin of Walter White's *Flight*. Or, consider the fairly common tendency, exemplified very well in this same *Flight,* for Negro novelists to have conceptions beyond their capacities. Or, to make an end of this, recall what a gratifying thing can happen when the conception and the capacity go hand-in-glove, as they do in William Gardner Smith's *Last of the Conquerors,* where the particular version of irony conceived by Smith, the irony of a Negro boy finding democratic treatment in an experience of life where he least expected it and which he cannot retrieve, is given just the right pitch by the elegiac tone that Smith gets immediately and sustains admirably in spite of the delicacy of its adjustment.

All around us today the air resounds with calls to integrate the Negro into our national life. Very probably the increasingly favorable reaction to those calls is a sign that both America and its Negroes are reaching a certain maturity. Negro writers are promising to do their bit in keeping pace with the latest trend. Symptomatically, they are losing, as never quite before, their exaggerated self-consciousness. Gwendolyn Brooks's *Satin-Legs Smith* represents without apology the South Side of Chicago, but none of his unabashed local color prevents him from representing very well also the diminution of man as a romantic spirit in the machine-made monotony of the modern metropolis. Redding's *Stranger and Alone* is a study of Uncle Tomism, but a study of Uncle Tomism that illuminates *sub specie aeternitatis* the ubiquitous errand-boys for Caesar. The Negro writer, who has always been very American, even in his failings and despite his handicaps, is still responsive to his environment. But there is still too little evidence that Negro criticism developed by literary scholarship is making strenuous efforts to "integrate" itself with any American pattern. For the pattern of American scholarship requires, if nothing else, some activity. We have sent by now a goodly squadron of students to the great graduate schools of America. We are even opening up now graduate schools of our own. Perhaps it may be argued in extenuation of our inertia as productive scholar-critics that our teaching loads are too great and our facilities for research too meager to permit us to do those things that we are really chagrined to leave undone. The argument is objectively sufficient. It faithfully describes current conditions as they statistically are. It is subjectively specious. For it says nothing about our will to change those conditions. It says nothing about our determination to see that integration in American education will mean not only the one-way traffic of Negroes going to white schools, but also the Americanizing in terms of budgets, curricula, physical plants, labor practices, administrative attitudes, and scholarly proficiency of Negro schools so that we may reasonably cherish the hope of finding, in some not-too-far-distant day, a fair amount of people who will want a two-way pattern of integration that will let whites come to "Negro" schools. And, above all, it says nothing about our resolution to do as much as we can under present conditions to integrate our own literature into the national consciousness.

There is really for us no true absolution. We have shirked overmuch our job. In 1945 *Phylon* published a poem by Robert Hayden called "Middle Passage." It was, I thought, a fine poem. Its infinite riches deserve some extended comment. I have never seen a printed reference to it of any consequence. In *The Craft of Fiction,* Percy Lubbock notices admiringly Leo Tolstoi's handling of time in *War and Peace.* In that novel, Lubbock points out, we feel the passage of time in two ways. We are aware of its flow from day to day and year to year, bearing away, like a conveyor belt, the span of a person's life. But we are also aware of it as a cycle of generations, a wheel ceaselessly revolving, always taking some generation up, some generation down. Langston Hughes's *Not Without Laughter* is much less bulky than *War and Peace.* Yet in *Not Without Laughter* one finds this same double sense of time, just as one finds, virtually wherever one stops to analyze Hughes's performance here, casements opening out upon the expansive world of universal suggestion created by great art.

I have said that Negro literature is often execrable. But it is far from being so execrable as to deserve the extent of neglect in which we have allowed it to languish. Moreover, I have tried to show that it is frequently critically challenging; indeed I have hinted that now and then it may reward even the most demanding critic with a moment of rapture. Finally, I have indicated that in my own thinking about the relation of one thing to another in this complex world, I can plainly see the development of a criticism around Negro literature as an integrative factor of no little value for the growth of democracy in America. Actually I look forward to the day when a book about Negroes, if someone should chance then to isolate such another incidental group in our social order, will have about the same significance as John P. Marquand's *The Late George Apley* or A. B. Guthrie's *The Way West* have now. And I want us, as students and teachers of Negro literature, to have had our share in preparing for that day. I want us to have affected both the quality and the reception of Negro writing in such a way as to hasten that age of felicity. I would have us, indeed, feel toward the development of an energetic scholarly criticism within our own ranks a sense of knightly obligation. And I would add, for all those who see eye-to-eye with me, "a fair promise of better things"—even to an increase in one's own sense of being personally alive.

Largo
for
Adonais

COUNTEE CULLEN *died in 1946. He had been an Alpha. After he died, I was asked to write about him for the Alpha journal,* The Sphinx. *Understandably, it was the assumption of the person who approached me that I would compose a requiem for our departed brother, which, though not necessarily a eulogy, would still be the proper kind of notice to give to the passing of an Alpha as highly esteemed as Cullen deservedly was.*

I have forgotten what prevented me from completing what I had promised to The Sphinx. *It was surely nothing of great moment, and it surely did not involve any matter of high principle or any aversion on my part to doing as I had said I would.*

But preparing to write about Cullen took me back to read all — or, certainly, nearly all — that he had written. It affected me in other ways also. Some of the writers of the Harlem Renaissance I had come to know as personal acquaintances, in several instances as close friends. Cullen I never met, just as I never met, or saw, Yolande DuBois, his first wife. I would eventually meet his second wife. At Fisk, after Cullen's death, I was to have on the staff of the student newspaper, DuBois Williams, Yolande DuBois' daughter by her second husband. And, rightly or wrongly, I was to feel that I did have some special reasons for appreciating the kind of psychic being I would have sworn Cullen was. I believed I had grown up in a home much like the home into which Cullen was taken by his foster parents, the Reverend Frederick Cullen and his wife. I thought I knew exactly how Cullen felt at NYU and Harvard. I had talked with people, friends of mine, who had been Cullen's close associates. All of this led me to postulate a certain tragedy (if the term is not too grandiloquent) in Cullen's life, a tragedy widespread among Negroes of Cullen's class and time, who had, as it were, no place to go. Whites tended to resent them. And their relations with the so-called Negro masses were hardly ever "natural." In a sharecropper's cabin, for instance, or a store-front church in Harlem, or even at the juke-joints and other recreation places of Negroes like those in the fiction of a Zora Neale Hurston or a George Wylie Henderson — they were interlopers.

"Largo for Adonais," then, is a glaring example of an essay that does not tackle cleanly its real subject, the impasse of a class. I have long thought it interesting that Cullen, after the Renaissance, retreated largely into translation, erudition, and playing children's games (his poetry written allegedly by a cat). Cullen did not solve his impasse. His class did not and has not. Nor have the greatest causative factors for the impasse changed as much de facto *as* de iure.

"Largo for Adonais" appeared in the Journal of Negro Education *in the winter of 1946.*

⊱⊰

Countee Cullen was a serious artist. He deserves, therefore, a serious criticism. Furthermore he was, in staunch purpose at least, a crusader for the good society. Now whether the exact correspondences exist between art and society that Ruskin argued, the fact remains that neither a good art nor a good society can be erected on shams. Both must have in their basic element, truth as well as force. Both, moreover, are vital to our happiness — at this hour, indeed, it would appear, to our mere security, if not even to our bare survival. It follows, then, by a logic which, whether ruthless or not, is certainly inescapable, that in dealing with the problems of society and art there are no such things as polite lies; for nothing can be courteous that implies danger. It can be purblind; it can be vicious; it may be disastrous; but it can never be polite.

Cullen's passing is lamentable. He was in many good ways an exceptional individual, and he was, beyond any caviling, one of the very best artists yet to emerge from our American Negro community. But he was not good enough. He fell too far short of epic achievement. He himself said in *Caroling Dusk* that he wished "any merit that may be in . . . my work to flow from it solely as the expression of a poet—with no racial consideration to bolster it up." As a writer, or as a champion of a minority group, he could not, of course, have taken any other stand and been respectable. People who oppose segregation, as Cullen did, and everyone of us should, must fight it all down the line. As a poet, therefore, it was important to Cullen that his race should not bar him from a universal audience on universal terms. He who also once said of some apparently Tory folks— ". . . they do not know that you,/John Keats, keep revel with me too"—was right in his consciousness of our desperate need to think in absolutes. That way, and that way alone, lies the only road that can establish Negro artists upon significant positions in an enduring culture. For commercial success or for transient celebrity we can produce picturesque vignettes of what too many people would like to suppose our whole life is—a cute, though rather savage, exoticism. But in so doing we are guilty of high treason to our best, indeed, our only, hope. Or we can press, as Cullen did, toward the mark of a high calling, and be, at the very worst, as Cullen was, a failure whose constructive elements, particularly in his youth, justify sympathetic and attentive regard by subsequent artists with irreproachable aspirations.

What then has Cullen to teach us? Surely his grand strategy was a campaign against cultural isolationism, for he saw very clearly that the interaction of art and society was a fact, and an important fact. Moreover, on the issue of integration he did not reason too simply. He had grasped the distinction, given wide currency by Howard Odum, between regionalism and sectionalism, between local emphases that act centripetally, strengthening even while they diversify a cultural unity, and local emphases of centrifugal, and, consequently, separatist, effect only. Thus reasoning, therefore, he could quite properly identify cultural isolationism with sectionalism and define genuine regionalism as a desirable factor in a well-rounded national literature. His major premises, then, left apparently nothing to be desired. But his operations did; and the reasons, probably, are not far to seek.

To begin with, Cullen as a person was a paradox—indeed, with master irony, he was the very sort of paradox that proved most bitterly his central credo that segregation is not a law of creation. Largely reared in New York City as the foster son of a minister, schooled there, graduated Phi Beta Kappa from New York University, with a Master of Arts degree from Harvard, Cullen was—in spite of his insistence that "his chief problem has been that of reconciling a Christian upbringing with a pagan inclination" and his sincere, in so far as he was aware, nostalgia for what he considered African moods—a well-bred American Aryan with a bourgeois background. All his life, without being conscious of his affectation, Cullen was trying to pass for a Negro. One illustration will here have to suffice.

Cullen, there is no need for anyone to suppose with guile, was much preoccupied with the paganism he considered so much a part of himself that, as he put it:

> God's alabaster turrets gleam
> Too high for me to win
> Unless he turns his face and lets
> Me bring my own gods in.

Moreover, Cullen thought of this paganism as African, as an atavism that unmistakably determined his cultural descent. But the truth is that Cullen's paganism was no more African than Visigothic, both of which it was far too sophisticated to have been. His Africa was a seventeenth-century pastoral; his paganism, Pan in a witch-doctor role. As Granville Hicks, thinking of E. E. Cummings and his fellows, has pointed out, the college generation to which Cullen belonged produced in its artists aesthetes—gentlemen who, if the one of them quoted by Hicks to support his thesis can be believed, "had no interest in social problems . . . read Casanova in French and Petronius in Latin, discussed Pater's prose, and argued about the voluptuousness of the church and the virtue of prostitution." How Cullen encountered Casanova and Petronius, if he tarried with them at all, I do not presume to know (although, curiously enough, the number of Magdalens he romanticizes in his verse is one form of documentary evidence fitting him to Hicks's formula and allying him with Hicks's dilettantes), but that Pater would hardly have been distressed by the Africa configured within the "copper sun and the scarlet sea" can hardly be doubted. For this synthetic continent lay in an aesthete's realm, discernible, with appropriate vagueness only, through a misty atmosphere of neo-Hellenism. The spicy grove, the cinnamon tree, the throbbing drums, the "cruel padded feet treading out, in the body's street, a jungle track," how pleasant the sensations they could set atingle in the blood of an Oxford don sipping tea between snatches of easygoing talk in his tranquil study, or how sweet the shocks they could start in the nerves of a pale student pining, in his imagist's ivory tower beside the Harvard Yard, to be consumed in a hard gem-like flame.

By the 1920s the real black man's Africa was no secret. Marcus Garvey had too many bright uniforms, but still a closer view of it than any aesthete. He at least saw it, though with a tragically illiterate concept of economics and politics and in terms primarily rooted in its exploitation. But whoever looked at Africa clear-eyed could see it plainly for what it was, with its leprosy, its elephantiasis, its human and animal filth, its harsh native codes in the diamond mines of South Africa, its ghastly memories of Leopold's "free state" and of the older Goering's wholesale extinction of a people in the quondam German colonies, its lack of sanitation, of machinery, of capital, of leadership, of power, of knowledge, but not without hope and not, for all its want of an Isles-of-Greece or Land-of-the-Lotos glamour in itself or in anything it had ever been, without a past that could be reliably, yet movingly, interpreted.

But Cullen's paganism had no source in any Africa, present or past. Substantially there was no difference between it and the vision of the dark continent that a kindly disposed white man of Cullen's temperament would have concocted. Yet while Cullen's romantic glorification of a non-Nordic universe demonstrated in its terms how white he was, it did psychologically answer other purposes as a means of defense and escape. As a defense it was part of Cullen's answer to the extravagant code of insult directed by his own social order against any Negro's self-respect. Cullen's environment bombarded him with its derogations of everything black, studied affronts to his dignity, Jemimas on the billboards, Gold-Dust twins in the magazine advertisements, Stepin Fetchits on the movie screen, a scornful silence in the history books. So Cullen fought back. He found "pride in clean, brown limbs," and "a brown girl's swagger" giving "a twitch to beauty like a queen." Once at least he flailed out too blindly:

> Who lies with his milk-white maiden
> Bound in the length of her pale gold hair,
> Cooled by her lips with the cold kiss laden,
> He lies, but he loves not there."

> Who lies with his nut-brown maiden,
> Bruised to the bone by her sin-black hair,
> Warmed with the wine that her full lips trade in,
> He lies, and his love lies there.

Some men do feel that the blacker the berry, the sweeter the juice. On the other hand only in a moment when he was perplexed to the extreme could Cullen have forgotten that, if anything in this world is unpredictable, it is the way of a man with a maid. The hapless savagery of Cullen's denial that anyone could love a white woman is merely a crescendo note in his rebellion against racism's debasement of everything not white. It was just an obvious example of his defensive instinct operating not wisely, but too well. It was, that is to say, part of the pattern of resistance for the service of which he had invoked his curiously treasonable reproduction of the African past. And it was, under keen analysis, only a little less felicitous. For, like his creation of pre-colonial Africa, it represented emotion run riot.

Cullen's intellect was not on guard when he blasphemed the efficiency of white women as lovers. Neither was his vigilance as acute as one could wish in the business of making real and meaningful his nonwhite heritage. Yet here one must remember the strength of a vicious circle before he condemns too harshly. It would have required on Cullen's part no *tour de force* to find pregnant and localized symbols for the Western culture whose departure Eliot laments in "Gerontion." Who were the heroes Cullen could name? Theseus, Ulysses, Jason, Aeneas, Siegfried, Beowulf, Roland, Arthur, Galahad, Tristram, Robin Hood, William Tell. What places chimed rich echoes in his legend-making memory? The Troad, the isles of Greece, *Mare Nostrum* and imperial Rome, Camelot, Lyonnesse, perhaps a northern castle ringed with fire. The white man's myths were, willy-nilly, an integral part of Cullen. Could he match the names he had learned in New York, at Harvard, in Europe, with similar symbols from African tradition? Why is his Africa no closer to the Congo than Sicily? Why are the terms in which he seeks its recapture so lacking in concreteness? Why are they the stock images only of the literary artificer? When Robert Frost mends a wall or picks apples in New England the right touch is there, the particular conclusive detail, putting the signature of authenticity upon this Yankee world, but whatever tricks Puck might try upon Shakespeare's groundlings they were not fooled. They knew they were in English Arden, not in an Attican grove. And, in spite of Cullen's noble purpose, name his world what he will, it, too, is still his cultural homeland, a province built, like Keats's "realms of gold," from the matter of bards who reign in fealty to Apollo.

The revolt in Cullen's paganism is, then, a revolt in name only. As such it leaves much to be desired. It is an ironic debacle, a case of fighting fire with fire. As a defense mechanism it is hoist upon its own petard, and as an escape device it ends, like all escapist literature, demobilized in a *cul de sac*. Of course, however, to charge Cullen with escapism, or more precisely, with undue escapism (since, obviously, a certain amount of release from this world is an inevitable gratification of artistic enterprise) is to raise something of an issue. For Cullen was an earnest worker. He was no poseur, and, let it never be forgotten, he was not, despite anything that might be said against him, a disreputable artist. Along with a felicity in graceful phrasing and a knack for endowing his verse with an elegant tone, he had high purposes of great value. He wanted Negroes accepted into the human family as casually as other people. As a part of that program he wanted to point up the fact that Negroes, too, have dignity and other favorable qualities. Yet he did not want Negroes stereotyped only as objects of noble pathos either. Quite deliberately he kept these intentions in the forefront of his consciousness. And so the Topsys and the Emperor Joneses are not typical of Cullen's work. Indeed much of his poetry is not "racial" at all. A decade before Frank Yerby's *The Foxes of Harrow* (in 1935, to be exact), Cullen had published his *The Medea and Some Poems;* and in 1940 his delightful little fancy, *The Lost Zoo*, with its Squili-liligees, Lapalakes, Ha-Ha-Has, Pussybows, Hoodinkuses-With-the-Double-Head, or Just Hoodinkuses, and their extinct associates, reminded the reading public that even Negroes are capable of pure, pointless, winsome fun. His themes also had the catholicity which his opposition to cultural isolationism implied. If he wrote of brown girls' love he also wrote of love as Robert Herrick or Sir John Suckling would have done; indeed, with even less of local color than these unregenerate Britishers, he pleigned of desire and the sense of loss, of the delights lovers find in being together, of the praise of love and of the anguish that accompanies the recognition of its cruelty. It is true that his long poem, "The Black Christ," is a poem of racial protest, but his equally ambitious "Medea" is no more a case of special pleading than its name suggests. In many ways, therefore, Cullen's impulses and his achievements were both estimable. Withal, it should not be overlooked to what extent Cullen was a pioneer and, as such, a person of resolution, integrity, and independence. Surely in doing many of his pieces he was intending to crack a tradition—the same tradition that says, for example, that all Negro sociologists must be experts on the black belt, or that all Negro singers must close their programs with a group of spirituals. In other words, in one respect at least, Cullen was a literary statesman rather than a literary politician, for the politician would have considered his market with a crafty callousness beyond Cullen. All these endearing qualities Cullen had. Yet he also had a taste for beauty as beauty, and this returns us to the escapist element in his poetry.

The aesthetic bias in Cullen is perhaps less noticeable because, according to the calendar at least, he belongs to our generation. Actually, although he probably thought of himself as having preeminent affinities with Keats, Cullen's milieu seems a curious blend of the seventeenth and eighteenth centuries (in England, not Africa or America). Poetry, as Elizabeth Drew and John L. Sweeney persuasively outline its history in their *Directions in Modern Poetry,* appears to alternate between periods of social and individual emphasis. The full-blooded Elizabethan Age was a time when literature was a highly social product. The seventeenth-century reflex was a poetry equally individual, in which the great preoccupations were love and religion, both matters primarily personal. Neo-classicism reflected the corporate disposition of its age. The Romanticists returned again to a major concern with the isolated ego. What were Cullen's abiding interests if they were not love and religion? Sometimes the love might take the form of hate; sometimes the religion might be paganism or aestheticism. Love and religion they still are. Again, did not Cullen prefer the tested diction, the familiar rhythms? Does he not also have his evidences of sensibility and sentimentality? These date his lyricism closer to Samuel Johnson's standards than to the Romanticists, though this might not be a judgment

in which Cullen himself would concur. Be that as it may, however, the fact remains that the aesthetes of Cullen's generation
are, by and large, experimentalists in radical styles. Whereas
Cullen's sense of form is altogether orthodox, their craving
after sensations enjoyable to themselves often shows itself in
arresting patterns. The poetry of E. E. Cummings, for instance,
is the poetry of a man whose aesthetic predispositions have
much to do with the organization of his expression in a manner disturbingly revolutionary to conventional people. The
dialogue of Ernest Hemingway is famous for its preoccupation
with form, its concern for squeezing into the way the thing is
said every possible characteristic overtone, and famous also
for its marked stylistic departure from the old school. It would
be a gross reader, indeed, who did not immediately become
aware of Cummings' spectacular deviations from the norm in
his handling of punctuation, word arrangement, typography
itself, or of the simplicity *sui generis* of Hemingway's dialogue
and his narrative style. Yet that same reader might never think
of Cullen as a writer whose appetite for form got the better of
him to a degree in which it did not ultimately damage the out-
put of these other two.

The plain truth is that Cullen never had too much to say.
Measure him as he himself has suggested, with an absolute
yardstick. Try him against the major poet with whom he connected himself, with Keats, and cast up the account. Keats's
absorbing preoccupation was with an issue as old as the hills—
truth, beauty, mutability, reality, epistemology, ontology. State
it how you may, men have been puzzling over this question of
the real versus the specious since memory runneth not to the
contrary. They still are, of course, and even now, as any
sympathetic reader of Wallace Stevens will hasten to testify,
continue to say important things about it. Nevertheless "La
Belle Dame Sans Merci," though it has fallen on the evil days
of dutiful classroom *translation* into literally true vernacular,
remains a major attack upon the cult of glamour, just as its
concomitant "Ode to a Nightingale" remains a major affir-
mation of the values beyond glamour's futility. Cullen's "Heri-

tage" is an attack on racism. But does it argue against racism as effectively as "La Belle Dame Sans Merci" attacks false standards? It does not. It lacks the plurisigns in which Keats spoke. Keep rereading it and it shrinks. The bitter-edged satire of its closing couplet is the right kind of a *coup de grace, corto y derecho,* short and straight. It stands up under pressure, but the rest of the poem largely goes bad, leaving nothing in the couplet's support. "Sweeney Among the Nightingales" is a poem famous for the success with which T. S. Eliot creates and maintains throughout it the required atmosphere of foreboding, so that when, at its end, through the agency of the nightingales Eliot links together the vulgar nonentity, Apeneck Sweeney, with the great Agamemnon in a brilliant play upon the colonel's-lady-and-Judy-O'Grady theme, the effect is tremendous. The whole short lyric is a mighty unit, all the pieces of the orchestra preparing the final consummation. And in "La Belle Dame Sans Merci," also, Keats does not release a word in error. His problem is to build up in his reader's consciousness, more through overtones than otherwise, a sense of the sort of beauty that ought to be repudiated. He wants his reader to have the intimate, absolute knowledge of this treasonable beauty that comes out of feeling it, not by definitions. So Keats's poem is a perfect metaphor made up of subsidiary metaphors all directed to one end, to make real in the terms of art, through a blending of sound with imagery and movement, Keats's concept of the nature of the loveliness that deceives.

But in "Heritage" the parts hardly fit. The images resolve themselves, upon analysis, into the pretty and irrelevant confections that they are. There is no way to make them tonally acceptable to the mood of satire that the situation demands. And just as there is no logic by which the moods of this poem can be synthesized, so is there also a fatal schism in the argument. Cullen, in his use of the African background, seems to be saying essentially, "Look out. I am savage. At any time the real me may burst through this veneer and run amok." But, to say that the heathenism in America is dangerous because it challenges the heathenism in his past is not merely to cheapen the terms of his theme, but also to blunt the appeal of his satire. His "strong bronzed men" and "regal black women" at least are in the right church, for his success as a polemicist. They are obviously meant to imply a fineness, a self-respect, and a self-sufficiency in the African culture that would properly explain and justify his rebellion against the white man's attempts to degrade Cullen for his black ancestry. They build Cullen up properly as a creature of royal lineage for whom only royal treatment is mete. But far too much of the material in "Heritage" will neither in sound nor in sense support this good motif. A considerable portion of the poem, on the other hand, is a technicolored jungle that bears substantially the same relation to the real Africa of slave-trading days as Longfellow's delightful Indian preserve—another literary kingdom in which, to borrow Van Wyck Brooks's apt characterization, there is only "the vague myth of a sunset land, a paradise in the West, where the mountains and forests were filled with deer and the lake swarmed with fishes"—bears to the actual pre-Columbian America.

Over Longfellow's happy hunting ground blew the Indians' gentle south wind, Shawondessa, a perfect symbol, not only in its zephyrous image, but even in its delicate luxuries of phonetics, for Longfellow's own genteel aestheticism. And it is Shawondessa, not the sand-bearing, throat-burning harmattan with its harsh implication of life's frequent rigor, which ripples ever so tenderly the pastel vegetation in Cullen's Watteau thickets. It is Shawondessa which passes "Where young forest lovers lie/Plighting troth beneath the sky." It is, indeed, this same Shawondessa, not true, unlearned, aboriginal, violent savagery that Cullen describes himself as feeling in

> . . . my sombre flesh and skin
> With the dark blood dammed within
> Like great pulsing tides of wine
> That, I fear, must burst the fine
> Channels of the chafing net
> Where they surge and foam and fret

or as moving

> Through my body, crying, "Strip!
> Doff this new exuberance.
> Come and dance the Lover's Dance!"

So when Cullen asks and answers: "Africa? A book one thumbs/ Listlessly, till slumber comes — " he has been honest about his own reaction. Africa has lulled him into sleep, an aesthete's trance, for ultimately the deliciousness of small sensations has captured everything in this poetry. If "Heritage" proposed to say something serious or important, or to develop moods consonant with the nature of its theme, those *desiderata* have in the act of realization been, surely unwittingly, forsaken. Cullen has escaped into the enchanted wood whence, undiverted, he can be rapt by the song of the nightingale. These verses cannot be justified by a reader searching in Cullen's poetry for the bread of life, but their tone-coloring is so sensuously worked in and the pictures that they make are such exquisite dreams. They are as escapist as that quatrain of his (in "Colored Blues Singer," not in "Heritage"):

> Such songs the mellow-bosomed maids
> Of Africa intone
> For lovers dead in hidden glades,
> Slow rotting flesh and bone,

where the swooning of the sound goes hand-in-glove with the pasteurization of the maids' bosoms and the euphemism of the corpses decomposing inoffensively in the fecund tropics. But escapism, even when it is as relatively innocuous as Cullen's aestheticism, has, in final terms, no positive values for the artist. The aesthetic surrender in "Heritage" constitutes a flight, not only from the real world with its complicated pattern of good and bad, its stench and maggots, as well as its "gentle flesh that feeds by the river brink," but also from the technical problems of the poem as a poem, its fusion of voices, its unity of context, its resolution of theme. So it indicates the general manner in which Cullen's aestheticism operated to his detriment, weakening his will, confusing and diluting his effects, turning him astray from the ends toward which he started. So also it leads us, together with his misconstrued paganism, into an understanding of the fact that neither intellectually nor artistically did Cullen possess the mastery without which an artist can never be truly sufficient. So it reminds us that Negro artists may fail on the universal world of art because of individual inadequacies as well as racial vendettas. And thus it carries us as a point of departure toward the consideration of an issue that leads beyond a concern with Cullen only or, for that matter, with any single writer, into a generalization which, sound or not, is certainly evangelical.

The disparity between Cullen's conscious aspirations and his real achievement is all too clear. What he most sincerely desired was a thing in itself right and good. He wanted to write poetry of such quality that it would be read and regarded highly as poetry, not charitably dismissed as "racial" literature. Yet Cullen had neither the intelligence nor the power to speak with superlative effectiveness either as Everyman or as "The Negro." But an artist's failures are by no means his own responsibility solely.

In her *From These Roots* Mary Colum examines the relationship of criticism to literature, particularly in the instance of a raw, still tentative and experimental culture such as America's, and, quoting Robert Lowell's well-known dictum, "We must have a criticism before we can have a literature," she makes a rather convincing demonstration that, whereas in old, established communities the artists and the people have a background of tradition that provides them with cultural poise, here we must discover what our tradition ought to be before we can create it and accept it. The literature does not, and should not, come first, with the critics following in its wake. The critics, with their revelations, their encouragement, their warnings, their guidance, should come first, and the literature should develop behind them into a tradition which not only the artists, but the critics, have had a hand in defining and creating.

If there is any substance in Miss Colum's thesis the question then arises: how did the critics discharge their obligation toward Cullen? Waiving the field, in so far as the white critics are concerned, what of the Negroes? Furthermore, what of the criticism in general written by Negroes in Cullen's time? If it is reasonable to hope that the generation to which Cullen belonged might, as Cullen himself wished to believe, produce Negro artists of universal rank, and if Miss Colum's priorities are not Sophistic, it is even more reasonable to expect, by this time, Negroes writing important criticism. For Cullen, it can well be supposed, the real test of an artist's stature was his ability to work on a level at which race was incidental—or at least no more exclusive a factor in the artist-audience relationship than George Santayana's Latinity, or Henry James's expatriation, or Keats's shortness. Very fairly this same criterion could serve as one good test of the progress of criticism (and literary scholarship, too, for that matter) among Negroes in America. Has any Negro done a work of general criticism, either for a comprehensive cultural entity or any discernible portion thereof (perhaps our own segregated element) as significant or as able (with all their limitations) as the late Vernon L. Parrington's *The Beginnings of Critical Realism in America* or Alfred Kazin's *On Native Grounds,* or even Van Wyck Brooks's one-dimensional New England studies? Moreover, since literary scholarship provides the firm base for informed criticism, out of the now not inconsiderable number of Negroes who have been going to school, many of them really quite competently, at America's best universities, has any one of them contrived a piece of inspired research like, let us say, *The Road to Xanadu?* Purely categorical answers to these questions might, in a merciful dispensation, be too extreme. Yet a fact is shadowed forth through this juxtaposition of Cullen and Negro criticism that ought to be baldly set out: Negro artists have done better in our culture than Negro critics. *Color* and *Native Son* have achieved a rank in the *belletristic geune,* which our critics, or critic-scholars, have not attained in theirs. And this is unfortunate. For, whatever the precise nature of the interaction of criticism and literature, surely a good healthy criticism is of invaluable service to any literature. Therefore, the development of critical writing by Negroes (though, it is to be hoped, not always about Negroes) is clearly in the nature of an imperative on our program.

Of course the Negro writing criticism finds himself immediately confronted with the anomaly that helps so much to make Cullen's poetry singularly interesting. The Negro critic does not want to be "racial," at least not in the sense that race is the be-all-and-end-all of his activity, or in that sense of separatism which sets up a double standard, actually a concession of inferiority on our part, in such a manner as to protect Negro artists from absolute measurements. Yet he does want to be "racial" in the sense of not shirking what he, unless he is a most curious Negro indeed, considers his obligation to do all that he can to improve the Negro's status. Really it seems so simple to see that these two objects need not be in conflict. Yet, even to an acute intelligence sincerely employed, they often seem irreconcilable.

Turn back to Cullen. I say that his self-knowledge as revealed in his poetry was woefully defective, and that, if he made any effort to think through the great problems of our time, that effort is not conspicuous in his verse. But certainly Cullen's mind was far above the average. So, apparently, was his integrity. It is true, admittedly, that Cullen never did too well at the business of satisfying both his racial patriotism and his immortal soul. To reveal his pride in his African ancestry and to make his audience know that pride as something he felt and justified, he defined the paganism that he declared was such a dominant factor in his reactions; and that paganism belied him with its non-African character. In such a poem as "Incident" where he was on firm ground, dealing with material that was actually part of his experience, his racism is admirable. Whenever, on the other hand, his racism was artificial, it failed him. Nevertheless, had Cullen been able to produce poetry that would have established him among the almighty of the ages, he would, of course, have resolved in the one irreproachable fashion his problem of serving jointly his race and his art. That he could not do, because his limitations as a personality — limitations that depended upon his composition as an individual and that would have rendered his poetry impotent and thin had he been a Scotchman or a Slav rather than an American of Negro extraction — made such a consummation impossible.

But Cullen did perceive clearly that the only way for a Negro to handle all his problems truly was in the constant quest of absolutes. It is interesting, moreover, to note that Cullen is most ridiculous and most futile when he surrenders to compromises with this perception. Take again his paganism. Can it be called dishonesty? Hardly. Can it be called corrupt? Somewhat. Can it be called valueless? Beyond all doubt. It would have been more useful for Cullen to have said to himself: "I do not know old Africa as well as I know old England, but I do know what it means to be alive in a minority group now, and in the light of that knowledge I will write better for everybody. I will unfold a plain, unvarnished tale and I will not try to create any formulas for my own self-gratifying deception or flight from the artist's obligation to see life wholly and truly. But Cullen blundered, albeit with the finest of intentions, into a defensive role that he was poorly equipped to maintain. The resulting debacle represents a fable for Negro critics in their handling of Negro themes (that is to say, in their criticism of the work of Negro artists). For the Negro critic dealing with his brother's product can succumb, also with the finest of intentions, to an illusion. Misguided by the doctrine of expediency, he can sacrifice literary statesmanship to literary politics. He can remember, for example, that Negro poets require encouragement in their own eyes and in the public's mind, and he may temper the rigor of his standards accordingly. Especially at this moment, when Negroes are just beginning their infiltration of the lands of milk and honey provided by best sellers, movie-bought novels, and Broadway hits, the critic may walk warily lest he indiscreetly disturb what might become a trend. He may, in other words, as Cullen did with an Africa of literary figure, see only the unrevolting aspects of the Negro product he reviews. But it is not good to do so. Aside from the practical consideration that best sellers flourish in a manner too complicated to be connected directly with criticism of any kind, there is the equally practical consideration, for persons whose idealism is not altogether counterfeit, that books may have, as John Dos Passos says, two kinds of extension, horizontal, through a few years, and vertical, through the ages. If there is to be a wave of best sellers from which Negro authors benefit commercially it will come, just as the wave of Graustarkian fiction came at the turn of the century, and if those best sellers are as superficial and as false in their qualities as the Graustark cycle, the wave will go with just the unpredictable waywardness of the Graustark wave.

Good criticism has never yet been master of the vulgar taste, or subject to it either, for that matter. Indeed to expect now, in an unfinished world, the same sort of consonances between informed, forthright literary criticism as those which exist between a successful candidate for political office and his electorate is to criminally oversimplify both the practices and the hopes of democracy. Public acclaim is not the business of criticism. Public enlightenment is. And while that enlightenment should be given in a manner that does not disregard the public's abilities, it should be none too keen about the public's, or the artist's, sensibilities. For criticism's real concerns are those of art itself: truth, beauty, goodness, these and the things like them that it is all too easy for the demagogue to rationalize into cheap cynicisms; and to serve *ars longa* is to serve a master more exacting, though immeasurably less fickle, than any public. The literary politician can recognize a thousand expedients demanding that criticism be wily and sycophantic and pliable, that is, *mirabile dictul,* follow the vogue. His vision is horizontal. But Negroes must beware the literary politician.

True, our politicians are usually thinking in terms of race patriotism. Their reflections are confused, not corrupt. Nevertheless they still land us where Cullen's paganism (another example of confusion) landed him — in a situation as spurious and finally as disastrous as Spenser's Bower of Bliss.

Some day some Negro, writing in America, will be the great artist for whose coming Cullen yearned. It is too early to say that that Negro is not writing now. It is not too early to say that, if he is writing, he has yet to do his definitive work. And it is far from too early to call, as Cullen did, for Negro writers accomplished enough to enter the mainstream of the Western world's literary tradition, and to call for critics equally full in their development. There are people who believe that the great American literature waits yet upon the future. There are others who wonder now if it will ever be written. They are thinking not merely of the atomic menace. They are thinking of other things — perhaps of the medieval synthesis, of the dignity it gave to man, the order it gave to his universe, the stable matrix it provided for his art. Perhaps, as Joseph Wood Krutch did in his *The Modern Temper*, they are placing against this synthesis our scientific cosmos and feeling that out of this impersonal welter of physics and psychology, no great literature, only a new barbarism, is possible. Perhaps they are looking, with James T. Farrell, at the consolidated control of the outlets for mass communication in America: radios owned by newspapers, Hollywood linked with book publishing, the reprint houses owned by the giants of the publishing trade, book-of-the-this-or-that clubs linked, also, like Hollywood and the reprint outfits, to these few big, gluttonous publishing octopi. Perhaps they see the smaller firms vanishing — publishing becoming big business, with all the nasty implications of such an outcome for expression in America. Perhaps, like many of our writers — Theodore Dreiser with his chemisms, Sinclair Lewis with his depressing villagers, Willa Cather, with her great souls — perhaps they are regarding contemporary man with compassion, sympathy, pity, but always with something of bewilderment and contempt. Perhaps they are pondering, like Arthur M. Schlesinger, Jr., the peculiar heightening of danger in periods after conflict: "Wars are generally not revolutions, especially when you win them. Thus the Civil War, like the two World Wars, diverted a good deal of energy and severed valuable continuities." And, thinking of severed continuities, perhaps they are hoping that this time only the right ones will be restored, lest the wrong revivals seal our doom.

But even the pessimists hope that this is the moment for the emergence of some new creative force. That kind of a force art can be. American literature, it is true, has hitherto expended most of its dynamics in protest and rebellion. Yet a century and a half ago Romanticism was a creative agent. Men had before them then, as they do always, problems of values, problems that artists can offer important contributions to solving. Still, not even the Napoleonic Era, disturbing as the implications of its industrial and political metamorphoses must have seemed, was in such desperate need of that understanding of itself, and its relations to the past and future that a great artist can provide, as is our own day. As everybody knows, the word *poet* means maker, and great artists create not just beauty, but things much more important for our lost, harassed epoch; they create senses of values, insights into what we and our world are, and hopes for what we and our world could or should become. Surely no one will deny that, if only as a response to our unprecedented mastery of our physical environment and our rapid and extensive abandonment of traditional beliefs and habits of thought, we need such insights now as never before. It does not matter, however, whether the creative interpretation of our culture comes from poet or critic. Granted Shelley's superlatives concerning the poet, the fact remains that the forms of art are many, and great criticism is an art in itself. It is an art, moreover, with the direct social bearing imperative from art now, for the complete critic must have, not only a feeling for art as art, but also a sense of history — or, to put it better, a creative philosophy, not merely for the future, but for the present instance. He must have, also, the integrity that comes from the capacity to live, even in an atmosphere of undramatic peace, always in that consciousness for the necessity of un- flagging valor and that horror of petty surrenders that most people can achieve only when destruction is the order of the day.

Whatever Countee Cullen's faults as a practitioner, he was altogether right in his devotion to absolutes. Historically his great value to the Negro community was his refusal to act, in so many ways, as Negroes were supposed to act. Still, from his *The Lost Zoo* or "The Medea" to *Alice in Wonderland* or *Samson Agonistes* is a great step. It is just as great a step from most of our criticism to a position like that accorded to Coleridge's *Biographia Literaria* or Taine's *History of English Literature.* But there can be no sooner day or hour for Negro criticism, whether its themes be of a special nature or not, to elevate its sights that far. Indeed for the Negro students of literature coming on, who read of Cullen and revere his memory, what better way could be found to decorate the tomb of Adonais!

The Ring
and the
Book

HUGH M. GLOSTER, *now the president of Morehouse College in Atlanta, founded an organization for the teachers of language and literature in predominantly black colleges before World War II. Originally named the Colored Language Association and usually known only by its familiar title of CLA, in the 1950s the organization officially became the College Language Association.*

"The Ring and the Book" was delivered by me at the banquet session of a CLA annual meeting. As I remember the occasion, the meeting was held in Atlanta probably in the spring of 1954. The essay appeared in 1955 in the CLA Bulletin, *the forerunner of the present official organ of CLA, the* CLA Journal.

Σξ

I cannot say exactly when I started reading Negro literature. I know I must have started as a boy—sometime before the Harlem Renaissance got into full swing—and I know that DuBois was my idol. I worshiped him. I must have read *The Souls of Black Folk* a dozen times. I never missed "As the Crow Flies" in the *Crisis*. Some of *Darkwater* I actually knew by heart.

Do you remember Nick Romano in Willard Motley's *Knock on Any Door*? And the effect the Mass had on him? The mutter of the Latin? The vestments? The flow of movement? The sense of beauty in it all that left the boy—for this was Nick as a boy—left him troubled with rapture and almost avid with desire to, as it were, follow the Grail. It is a way only the young can feel. It was the way I felt about DuBois.

63

That has been a fairly long time ago now. But I still remember the intensity of this, my first literary passion. I used to wonder then why more people did not know about DuBois. I meant everybody—not just the colored people who formed the omnipresent base of immediate reality in my world. I never seemed to find DuBois' name in the books and newspapers and magazines that made up my all-American experience of reading. I have had a quarter of a century, and more, to anatomize my wonder. I think I am beginning now to know some of the reasons for the situation that occasioned it. And those reasons are not altogether simple. They might have been had DuBois merely not been the writer I thought he was. He was not, and he is not, not without some grave reservations here and there, but he is still sound enough to have had a greater audience than he ever got. And great audiences do have a lot to do with the making of great poets. One really cannot talk about Negro writers in America without talking about the audience-author relationship.

Give the Negro writer his due. It is not whimpering and whining on his part when he says that this author-audience relation has been especially unkind to him. In his *The Novel and the Modern World* David Daiches considers early the problem of symbols for the imaginative writer. He knows, as you do, that not just words are symbols, but acts and situations. A character in a novel makes a certain gesture, says a certain thing, takes a certain course of action. Everything he does has meaning. It is part and parcel of the only true value the novel has, its value as a symbol in the connotative sense. It is part, that is, of the meaning associated not so much with a thing-in-itself as with the significance people attach to that thing.

To prove this point, Daiches uses an illustration some of you may be remembering at this very moment. He takes a case of seduction. When one thinks about it objectively one has to admit that seduction is, after all, just seduction—and has been through the ages. But Mr. Daiches transports his seduction through the conditioned reflexes of three centuries. The seduc-

tion does not change, but how its meaning does! The sentimental eighteenth century gushes tears over it. It feels,
deliciously, the plight of the victimized maid. The prudish
nineteenth century averts its eyes, in pious smugness, from the
unspeakable outrage. Its world could not abide such heinous
impropriety. But the blasé twentieth century takes the whole
thing in stride. As Mr. Daiches puts it, using an admirable
comparison, a seduction means no more to our epoch than the
drinking of a cup of tea.

Note, then, again something you all know, how much the
state of people's minds means to a symbol. And note, too, that
symbols are of service to a writer not so much because people
have individual responses to them, but because people tend to
belong to groups that, in Mr. Daiches' modest but competent
phrase, share a community of belief. Why, after all, can a
writer be reasonably sure that he will convey to others that
which he intends? Because people so often do not think for
themselves, but like everyone else. All of you have been to
college. All of you are humanists. I say, "the isles of Greece,"
and I am almost ready to wager on the troop of images that
start filing through your minds. There will be the Acropolis
and the Greek philosophers, Attic tragedy and the defeated
Persians, the gods of Olympus and the hexameters of Homer.
There will be other pictures, certainly a large percentage of
them as widely recurrent in this context as these. And there
may well be the figure of Byron, too, and the tag from him,
"Where burning Sappho loved and sung."

I need not tell you that there is, in the sweeping terms that
count most for the writer who wants all the public ear, a community of belief about Negroes in America. I remember that
for many years whenever I went to a movie I could never avoid
a sense of impotent fury every time I looked at one of Hollywood's prison scenes. Unfailingly, each penitentiary episode
had Negroes in it. They were always there, bigger than life and
stage center, where they absolutely could not be missed. Yet

the movies never seemed to feel that Negroes had any other place in America's communal activities. I would search the street scenes in those same movies, often with a sullen desperation. But, if what I was looking at was just an ordinary American crowd going about the ordinary business of civilized existence, peer as I might, the faces there were always unmistakably white.

The movies are changing now, for the community of belief about Negroes in America is changing. But our brave, new world is still far off, for it still means more in America to be a Negro than to drink a cup of tea. The gods have played a ghastly joke on Negro writers. What is it Countee Cullen once said?: "Yet do I marvel at this curious thing,/To make a poet black, and bid him sing." Part of Cullen's curious thing has been a rigorous act of thaumaturgy required of the Negro writer. He must say that Negroes are good to a community for which the very word *Negro* has, for such an extended period, been a symbol for almost everything bad.

An unfinished business, then, of the Negro writer is to widen the range within which his racial symbols can be used effectively with more regard for truth than for expediency. He cannot do this job alone. It is not that kind of a job. Many people and groups must help him, and in many ways; some of them must be literary, many of them decidedly otherwise. I firmly believe — and I know you join with me in this conviction — that no group should be more determined to come to his aid than ours. It is not only that Negro writing has got to be a major concern of ours. It is also that Negro writing has, since its inception, been something we have lived with. We know it, as no other single group of men and women does, perhaps better even than the people who wrote it. And so we know that, while much of Negro writing is bad, much of it is good, too, and virtually all of it can be interpreted for the improvement of the community of belief to which the Negro writer must appeal when he takes his product outside the market of his own race.

We know, for example, that almost never is Negro literature really read. Is it not amazing how much of the criticism of Negro literature by non-Negroes, as well as by Negroes, never seems to be really literary? Here is a white critic reading a standard white author. He takes him to pieces as an artist, gets dow into the work where he can run its very grains of substance through his hands and feel their texture. But rarely does a white critic go to such pains with a Negro work of art. Actually, most criticism of Negro literature represents essays in morals or sociology, whatever its trappings of jargon. It does not come from the study of a work of art primarily in terms that are artistic.

True, some people feel that it is better thus, that Negro literature cannot stand close artistic scrutiny. They are in grievous error. With a large portion of Negro literature it is possible to make as elaborate an analysis as one may choose, without finding the literature anything like disgraceful. You have read, no doubt, William Gardner Smith's *Last of the Conquerors*. That was a first novel that has now, within a very few years, dropped into virtual oblivion. If you have not done so recently, look at it again. Its form is beautiful. It is a work of irony, built around the incongruity of a Philadelphia Negro finding democracy in Occupied Berlin. To do this the novel sets up a three-world configuration. One world is life for this Philadelphia Negro, a soldier named Hayes Dawkins, in Berlin. A second world is life for him in another part of Germany, the Bremburg area, which is really a sort of concentration camp for Negro soldiers. The third world, never seen, but only reported in the flashbacks of various Negro soldiers, is life for Negroes in America. Through the agency of this configuration, *Last of the Conquerors* facilitates greatly the achievement of some interesting effects. In its pairing of world number one with world number three it achieves high burlesque. In its pairing of world number two with world number three it achieves low burlesque. For Berlin is to Dawkins a midsummer idyll, whereas Bremburg is, in some respects at least, worse than Philadelphia. Moreover, placing world number one first in the book casts over the whole performance a mood of wistful reminiscence and a sense of loss that conflates sweetly the author's irony with a tone of elegy. Through much of *Last of the Conquerors* Dawkins is looking back on a golden age, as for example Willa Cather looked back, first, upon the Nebraska of her girlhood and, later, on progressively more remote periods of the American past. Through much of it, that is, Dawkins is voicing a lament for vanished glory, singing the dirge in which the tears of things are even bitterer because things have once been better. And through all of *Last of the Conquerors* Dawkins is recording impressions of whatever world is around him with the special candor and simplicity attributed by tradition to the "average guy" who must be the hero in *ingénu* satire. The form of the book makes all these things possible, as well as some other things I do not now have time to mention. And there are other matters of sheer art that match the form in excellence. One could talk about them at length, but people almost never do. What other people have failed to do, we must begin to do on a significant scale. We must do it for the sake of our writers. We must do it for the sake of general truth.

For although a million and one forces must be brought into action to change the community of belief in America, we stand in a strategic position for the whole operation. Our perceptions are right when we assume that racial stereotypes in America can last only so long as white people do not know Negroes. Of course the best way for anybody to know anybody else is to know him in person, to actually have direct contact with him. But probably the second-best way for human beings to meet is through literature. If I cannot go to England and France, then I can know Englishmen by reading English authors. I can know Frenchmen by reading French authors. People who *really* read Negro literature have this same chance to get to know Negroes. And when they get to know the Negro as a goodly portion of our authors reveal him, they will be all the readier to change some of their prized beliefs about the nature of the Negro character.

As individuals we work at this job of bettering the climate for Negro symbolism every time we write a good article on Negro literature, a good review of some piece of Negro expression, a good book on what Negro authors have done with Negro material. But as individuals and as a group there is something else we must do. I have said this before. I say it again. We must affect the administration of the higher learning in the colleges where we teach. We must not do this pettishly. College administrators have no feud with us. But they carry no special brief for us either. After all they are men on whom a myriad of claims press down. Still it is our duty to tell them over and over that we need in our colleges research professorships in Negro literature, special library grants for Negro materials, publication subsidies for the work of Negro scholars and critics, lower teaching loads for many of us, and emoluments both for the body and the spirit that will make our interest in Negro literature less of a supererogatory chore than it has sometimes been.

I play this game with myself about Negro literature. I think of what has been written there as the book. I think of the community of belief around the book as the ring. And then I see the ring, tight as it is, encircling the book and constricting it within a pitifully small area. You see what we must do. You knew it before I started, but I do not therefore apologize. Because a thing has been said or thought before is no reason that it should not be said again, and even again and again. We need to work, in every way we can, at widening the ring. The book cannot really expand unless the ring does also. The Greeks had a River Ocean, which encompassed nothing less than the whole wide world. Our work in this association will never be done until our ring has lost all its boundaries and disappeared, finally, into that river.

A Word
About
Simple

LANGSTON HUGHES *and I, as well as Lang's close companion Zell Ingram, had formed a lasting friendship in 1931. Once, after Lang had started the series in which he created a new character, known as Simple, for a weekly contribution to the Chicago* **Defender,** *he and I talked rather long into the night, until his working time, about Simple.*

Lang liked to write at night. He slept in the morning, rose in the afternoon and entertained his friends, or did the other nonwriting things he wanted to do, until the rest of the world began to retire. Then he retired too, but to his desk, not to his bed. On the night when he and I reviewed Simple he was in the midst of a furious putsch *to finish a manuscript on which he was terribly late for his publisher. I took his reluctance to abandon talk of Simple, as well as his assurance that Simple had fulfilled his intentions more than most of his creations, as a sign of his satisfaction both with Simple as a work of art and with the response of the Negro public, at whom Simple had been aimed, to this character who bore, for this public, such a familiar store of words and deeds.*

I have a great respect for Simple. All readers, understandably, worry about the veracity, the truth to life, of characters whom they encounter in fiction. It seems to me that Simple is about as veracious as an imagined character well can be. I felt that I knew him because I felt that I had met his prototype in the flesh in every Negro community in which I had ever been. He lacks the grandness of projection of an Invisible Man. In such a lack, indeed, he is simple. Yet, strong as is his attachment to a particular genus of Negro in a particular habitat and era, Simple is not too simple. There are overtones in Simple that permit him to transcend the local and to touch upon universal complexities.

"A Word About Simple" was prepared for a 1968 issue of the CLA Journal *devoted to Langston Hughes as a memorial to him and his literary achievement. The essay was then included in Therman O'Daniel (ed.),* Langston Hughes, Black Genius: A Critical Evaluation *into which this special issue of the* CLA Journal *was expanded.*

☓

It is highly probable that Langston Hughes reached his most appreciative, as well as his widest, audience with a character whom he named, eponymously and with obvious relish, Jesse B. Semple. The *Jesse,* not too incidentally, clearly invited an abbreviation to *Jess.*

Simple, as Simple was called, made his bow to the world in the columns of the Chicago *Defender,* the Negro weekly which, in its heyday from early in World War I through the whole of World War II, circulated into virtually every nook and cranny of Negro America and, indeed, functioned as a sort of bible to many Negroes in every walk of Negro life. Via the columns of the *Defender,* then, Hughes addressed not so much the Negro elite, cultural or otherwise. Rather, he spoke, powerfully and directly, to the very Negro of whom Simple was supposed to constitute an almost perfect replica. He spoke, that is, in great part, to the black rank and file of our industrial Babylon, who may not have been nearly so illiterate as his slave forebears, but who even now is still a far cry in his rapport with the world of books from the proverbial Harvard graduate.

Illiterate or not, however, these Negroes, a twentieth-century equivalent of Chaucer's fair field full of folk, seem to have taken Simple to their hearts. They followed him week after week in the columns of the *Defender.* They gossiped about him with their associates. They found Simple understandable and comfortably convincing. True, they had not created Simple from an impulse originating in their own minds, not made him what he became through arts they had learned to practice, as, for instance, an earlier epoch of folk Negroes had created and then, in effect, composed the Negro spiritual. In these senses, but only in these senses, Simple lacks the full authenticity of folk material. He was an adopted child, not a native son. Yet the attitude of his foster parents, the often so-called "common, ordinary" Negroes, toward him, their ready identification with him, suggests a special status of importance for his significance. Whether or not he is truly like most ordinary Negroes, he is certainly, in both form and substance, what many ordinary Negroes were at least once prepared to concede without rancor that they thought they were. At least, to that extent, Simple must be accounted a folk Negro's concept of the folk Negro. Thus, too, he must be seriously considered a valuable specimen of Americana.

As such, it may well be noted first of Simple that he is a colored man, a highly visible Negro with a skin too dark, facial features too African, and hair too anything but lank, to be mistaken for an Aryan. He comes from Virginia, though in the days of his youth, when the Solid South (an admirable figure of speech) was still intact, there were localities in Virginia as dismaying to Negroes as the worst counties in the heartland of the Old Confederacy. After a childhood in which he was, in his own words, "passed around" among his relatives—for, of his actual parents, he clearly never had much knowledge—he has gravitated to Harlem, with intermediate stops, during one of which he has married and "separated," that have qualified him for a true insider's view of a big-city Negro ghetto. Under the perspective of *multum in parvo*, indeed, his personal history typifies in several vital respects the sociological Negro of his class. He is the product of a broken home, out-migration from the South, and a disillusioning experience as a young and naively hopeful husband.

Put in the context of the environment forced upon him, Simple's efforts to express himself through the spoken word could hardly be expected to emanate from a well of English undefiled. As a matter of inescapable fact, he speaks a dialect. It is not that curious idiom, in which pronouns converted into "dises" and "dats" play a conspicuous role, so long associated with the synthetic Negro of blackface minstrelsy and the, until most recently, orthodox American dogmas about Negro behavior. That idiom seemed determined to maintain the proposition that Negroes could not master the approved pronunciations of some English sounds—either (or both) because of innate biological inadequacies in the organs of speech solely and irremediably attributable to the Negro's African blood, or (if not and) because the Negro ear, in its neurological inferiorities, simply could not properly hear the nuances of sound imparted to speech by a white tongue. But Simple talks as he does plainly because he has not had the benefit of living during his formative years where the people closest around him would have provided him with models of impeccable utterance. Nor has he had later much institutionalized linguistic aid that could have served as a corrective. In his own superbly succinct solecism, he has not been "colleged." He says usually (though, puzzlingly enough, not invariably) "I were" for "I was." It is as if he has somehow established in his mind both an awareness of the interesting intelligence that verbs should be conjugated and an inclination so special to show his eagerness to comply with civilized procedures that he overdoes his willingness to inflect. Moreover, as with his peers whom one may encounter in such fictive haunts as those of *Invisible Man*, he has also a taste, as well as a positive knack, for either coining, or remembering, locutions that rhyme as they quip and that, in addition, are great fun to be savored as they parade over, and roll around, the tongue.

He spends, for instance, the infrequent freest of his free time with a party-loving voluptuous vixen who is "loose as a goose,"[1] strictly an "after-hours gal,"[2] and "great when the

---

1. Langston Hughes, *Simple Takes a Wife* (New York, 1953), 221.
2. *Ibid.*, 47.

hour is late, the wine is fine, and mellow whiskey has made you frisky."[3] His Cousin Minnie—who explodes upon him from an obscurity into which, once he is forced to contemplate her face and physiognomy, he would gladly consign her again at least until the Resurrection—seems to him to have taken as her motto what she does, incidentally, once proclaim to him in no uncertain terms as the first principle of her existence: "beg, borrow and ball till you get it all."[4] Reflecting mournfully on the course of young love as he has often observed it in the ghetto, Simple intones, "Midsummer madness brings winter sadness, so curb your badness."[5] Yet, in a moment of his own ebullience he can, with a vulgarity unusual for him (though he is speaking really in an aside and not to the lady in question), command a passing female whom he does not know, but whose figure agreeably astonishes him: "Baby, if you must walk away, walk straight—and don't shake your tailgate."[6]

Simple, in short, is a character who would clearly be something of a bull in a china shop in those purlieus of America frequented by the so-called best people. Nevertheless, even at his very worst he represents a great departure from the stereotypes of the Negro traditionally afloat in the common lore of the American mass intelligence. He is not Little Black Sambo grown up and existing half-wittedly in an urban setting beyond his resources to cope with; nor is he a brute, a demented ape-man with a fearful affinity for lust and pillage, especially apropos the bodies and properties of persons more Nordic than himself. Indeed, quite to the contrary, he is an *ingénu*, with very decent instincts, and a ruffian only in the sense that he is, underneath his gaucheries and his shortcomings, a diamond, unpolished and sometimes uncut.

He has, as has already been implied, reached maturity with little guidance after a childhood in humble circumstances. He

3. *Ibid.*
4. Langston Hughes, *Simple Stakes a Claim* (New York, 1953), 90.
5. Hughes, *Simple Takes a Wife*, 92.
6. *Ibid.*, 101.

did sojourn in Baltimore long enough, as we have also seen, to have become involved with the wife from whom he has been estranged for a considerable time. His serious and sustained interest in the likable nice girl whom he is determined to wed, once he has secured the divorce, the cost of which somewhat appalls him, testifies to his fundamental kinship with the Tom Joneses, rather than the Blifils, of this world. His vices might perturb an Anthony Comstock. They would hardly perturb an apostle of sweet reasonableness. He drinks a nightly beer. When he can get it, he is not averse to stronger stimulant. But he is, except on the rarest of occasions, only a mild inebriate, his addiction being controlled both by his disposition and his purse. On the other hand, to speak the utter truth, he is also a great cadger of drinks, principally from the college-bred associate who is his boon companion at Simple's most accessible version of the Mermaid Tavern.

Even so, however, his addiction to the bottle, such as it is, is actually only the indulgence of a comradely spirit. At the bar, with the excuse of a slowly diminishing glass in his hand, and an attendant ear at his side, he assumes the role of genial philosopher which is his *metier*. For bitterness has not corroded him as it has a Bigger Thomas or a Rufus Scott. It is a human comedy that Simple passes in review in his castle of indolence at his Harlem rendezvous, not an unrelieved panorama of hopeless gloom and horrors. In Simple's world, things sometimes happen for the best, all too often for the worst—though there is a tendency for the good things to come to good people just when the bad things are about to become unbearable; and always, for the common lot of man, the good and the bad are tempered, and their deviations in any direction mediated toward a neutral ground, by laughter, the superb and therapeutic acknowledgment by the human intellect that frailties of many kinds are endemic to the human condition.

Nor is Simple's laughter an assault on others. It is, like his petty bibulousness, companionable. He laughs with his fellows, at their foibles and at his own. When he recounts his wooing of his wife and the subsequent gradual disintegration of his marriage, he is at least as much the target of his own satirical thrusts as anyone else. When his young cousin just out of high school, Franklin D. Roosevelt Brown, as much a bolt from the blue as the Cousin Minnie to whom reference has already been made, appears to discomfit him momentarily, and then to win his only apparently grudging approval, it is his own slack habits that Simple reviews for exposure to good-humored ridicule as much as his young cousin's impetuosity. Moreover, as it does develop that he rather likes playing the role of a father, or an older uncle, to his young kinsman, and even that he plays both roles rather well, the sardonic self-deprecations with which he dismisses his virtuous behavior confirm the verdict of his relations with the girl who is his intended — that he is essentially made of the salt of the earth, that his deeper instincts substantiate democracy's trust in the average man, that he even has dreams, big dreams of a noble nature, which, if he cannot always articulate them, or even admit publicly to their possession without some embarrassment, still are, after all is said and done, the things to which he truly clings.

Hughes with Jesse B. Simple is not, as is well known, the first Negro writer to write about the Negro folk. Long before Simple, to take a justly conspicuous example, James Weldon Johnson in *God's Trombones* renders old-time folk-Negro preaching into verse, a medium he may well have chosen in the hope that it would impart to his black divines a longer and happier literary life, especially since the verse is not in dialect. Johnson probably wanted his preachers to be admired. For, just as Johnson expressly felt that the great wide world of conscious cultural recognition had failed to give due credit to the Negro spiritual, so he was correspondingly distressed at this same world's neglect of the art of the old-fashioned Negro preacher — an art which, moreover, he could see was being contained within an epoch in Negro history that would not, and, indeed, could not, last. Johnson, then, with his preachers, was an advocate, not so much of the mere existence of a phenomenon, as of a theory maintaining its special worth. But Hughes wanted Simple merely to be known. At the very heart of American racism there seems to be an assumption of the most dangerous import: to wit, that there are no Negroes who are average people. This assumption for a long time exercised great sway over virtually all the American contemplation of Negro life. All Negroes were exceptional. A few, like Booker T. Washington in his time, and Ralph Bunche later on, were exceptionally intelligent, usually because, probably, of an admixture of white blood. Also beneficent — and more understandable since intellect is not the decisive factor for performing artists, but rather some peculiar organic or neurological accidents — were freaks like Blind Tom and Marian Anderson, Negroes who could play and sing not only their own simple Negro songs, but even compositions from the classical literature of serious music. But whether Negroes were tragic mulattoes or curious developments from their usually somewhat defective African genes, in the final analysis, they were all freaks, even when of a beneficent kind.

Most Negroes, however, were not freaks of a beneficent kind. They were departures from nature in their lack of normal human attributes. So read, and still reads, the holy writ of American racism. Moreover, by an unfortunate coincidence, so read, in effect, the pronouncements of most Negro writers on Negro subjects. In all of Negro fiction the Negro who is unabashedly and simply an average man is as rare as once, in that same fiction, octoroons were disturbingly numerous. The best-known Negro novels, even *Invisible Man* (as, however, its title implies) abound with grotesques, with people who do not act normally and whose distinctive stigma is failure, so that the prevailing conclusion to a Negro's tale of Negro life is catastrophe — Bigger Thomas awaiting execution, Lutie Johnson fleeing the corpse of the would-be seducer she has just murdered, Bob Jones (protagonist of *If He Hollers Let Him Go*) on his way to enforced military service, the Invisible Man submerged, and lost, in his hole in the ground.

The motives of the Negro writer, of course, have not been those of the white supremacists, nor has the chain of reasoning by which he has arrived at his conclusions been that of white supremacists. Negroes have been maimed, the Negro writer has contended, by their environment. The Negro characters of the Negro writer are freaks, pitiably and depressingly so, say their Negro creators, because the superimposed conditions of Negro life make them what they are. Their environment is freakish. How can they be otherwise? Yet, the plain truth is that men have never conclusively resolved the conundrum of the true influence of adversity upon the human psyche. And, moreover, most Negroes in actual life are not awaiting execution, fleeing murdered corpses, or living in subbasements either for ritual or fiscal reasons of an imperative nature.

What, then, are Negroes really like? This is the question Langston Hughes seems to ask with his portrait of Simple. And his reply seems to be altogether different from many of the chilling responses to that same question provided by the apostles of a belief in the Negro *manque.* Thus, in Hughes's warm and sane definition of an average Negro, Simple is no freak. He adores Jackie Robinson and respects Ralph Bunche, but he is no superman like either of them. Simple is an ordinary person who happens to be a Negro. He has an understandable distaste for white people who abuse him merely because he is a Negro or who commit acts that contribute to the system that exists solely to perpetrate a continuing series of such abuses. On the other hand, he takes also a dim view of the nastiness often observable in Negroes. His landlady, he has noted, is no angel of sweetness and light and, indeed, he scathes a Negro girl who is clerking in a white chain store for her rudeness and incompetence, quite as much as he does President Eisenhower for spending so much time playing segregated golf in segregated Georgia.

To Simple, quite obviously, the millennium is far, far in a distant future. His vision of the good life is a modest conception only remotely related to the heady doctrine of the perfectibility of man, as articulated, let us say, by such an evangelist of a new order as a Shelley or a Fourier. It is based upon a soberly realistic acceptance of human society in which due allowance is made for man's limitations as well as for his potential for self-improvement. Nor is Simple unique in the art of Langston Hughes. Rather he is representative. He belongs to the same world as the Negro characters, more memorable for their ordinariness than anything else, in Hughes's one novel, *Not Without Laughter*. For Hughes never succumbed to the monstrous error of arguing that, because race prejudice is itself monstrous, it has made Negroes monsters.

American history proves Hughes right. In the 1860s, there were some prophets who debated the potential length of time during which Negroes, freed to use their own resources, could manage even physical survival in the complex American environment. Some of these critics wondered, indeed, if the American Negro might not be extinct by the end of the nineteenth century. The nineteenth century has been gone almost seventy years. At Emancipation, speaking generously, there were less than five and a half million Negroes in America. In the 1960s, speaking cautiously, there are at least four Negroes extant for every Negro alive when President Lincoln issued his history-making Proclamation. Moreover, gradually, and in spite of an occasional setback here and there, it has become unmistakably clear that the general direction of Negro well-being in America is upward. The Negro has survived, multiplied, and improved his American status in every respect.

He will never, however, be perfect. Nor will America. Most Americans in the twenty-first century, as now, heretofore, and forever hereafter, will continue to be average personalities. They will still, to an extent, get divorces, waste time with light women, drink beverages stronger than tea, lose an occasional job, mistreat their fellows, shirk responsibilities, and commit crimes against the state and nature. But they will also, and probably to a relatively greater degree, sometimes fall ecstatically, beautifully, and nobly in love, aid their relatives, do good turns for friends and, now and then, even for strangers; and, at some rare, unforeseen, and, to them, unavoidable moments, they will even rise above themselves to perform prodigies of heroism and gracious feats magnificent in their altruism. Black and white, that is, they will be like Simple. Thus, they will justify, as they demonstrate, Langston Hughes's faith in human nature and illustrate the soundness of his affirmations about Negroes, America, and humanity in general. These future Americans, that is, will join the Negro readers who, when Simple did appear in the *Defender,* rallied round him in such a manner as to indicate their conviction of his reality. They will give further incontrovertible proof, in their sentiments as well as their conduct, of the validity of Hughes's judgments on his chosen subject, the true character of the Negro Everyman. They will vindicate, in fact, the basic implications of our political and social creeds in America, which argue that governments and communities exist not for the privileged few, but in the interest of everyone—even, and indeed most, for the Simples of this earth.

The Case
for
American Negro
Literature

IN *1950, when "An Essay in Criticism" appeared in* Phylon, *America was a segregated world, how completely segregated I believe it would be difficult today to convey to Americans under thirty. By 1955 the Supreme Court had already issued its landmark Brown* vs. *Topeka decision. But if the decision was working, if segregation was being eliminated, no ordinary observer could have been aware of it.*

It is tempting indeed to compare the Eisenhower years with the two Grant administrations. Both Eisenhower and Grant were military heroes who were elected to the American presidency not too long after wars in which each of them had captured the popular imagination and not long, either, in both cases, after what amounted to, for Negroes, emancipation proclamations. But neither Grant nor Eisenhower gave strong executive support to emancipation. Looking back now on the Eisenhower years it is almost impossible not to think of steps which the Eisenhower administration could have taken to lead the country toward integration. There could at least have been task forces, to give advice and stimulate action. But even such task forces were never appointed. In 1954 and 1955 we could not, of course, foresee Montgomery and Little Rock or the shape of the sixties. But we could, and did, if we believed in integration, bewail President Eisenhower's proclivity, where integration was concerned, to be content with a program of laissez faire, which in our judgment amounted to a policy of supporting segregation.

The opening of the essay "The Case for American Negro Literature" partially portrays an actual incident. A group of college teachers, two

from Vanderbilt, one from the University of Tennessee, and about half
a dozen from Fisk, were gathered around a table in an establishment,
since burned down, called the Waikiki. It is somewhat significant that
the Waikiki, a restaurant and lounging spot for academic types, was
near the Fisk campus. In 1955 people still lived in an America where
it was practicable for whites to be at ease with Negroes in Negro
surroundings, but difficult, if not dangerous, for Negroes to be similarly
at ease with whites in a "white" place of "public" accommodation.

All of us in the Waikiki believed in integration. Our mood, our
deep convictions, our momentary setting in the Waikiki, and especially
the atmosphere and temper of America during that long lull after the
Supreme Court decision and before anything really happened, provide a
frame of reference that may well be indispensable, in this later day, for
the reception of "The Case for American Negro Literature" that I
originally wanted.

This essay was printed in the Michigan Alumnus Quarterly
Review *in early 1955.*

⊱⊰

Not so long ago I was in a small party of college teachers when
the subject of American Negro literature came up. One of the
group, a mathematician from the University of Tennessee, and
a very likable fellow, quickly volunteered his belief that there
should be no such absurdities as courses in Negro literature. As
he saw it there had been enough shunting of the Negro off into
a corner. His theory was that American schools should merely
offer courses in American literature which did justice, without
fear or favor, to American Negro literature. And there they
should leave well enough alone.

Behind his theorizing was the fairest of motives. He was
thinking—there can be no doubt of his sincerity—of how
abominable an hypocrisy it is to give lip service, and lip service
only, to democratic idealism. There may have been a touch of
Jeffersonianism in his dialectic, too, compounded with a liberal
sprinkling of the sturdy spirit of old English yeomanry, which
asked no quarter, but, unsentimentally, gave none either.

Basically, however, his concern was for democracy as an upright faith proved by its good works rather than its unctuous sentiments. Besides (I continue to paraphrase him), segregation was beginning to pass. It was as if all over America the meteorological drama of *Ghosts'* closing scene was being enacted on a giant stage, with a fog lifting everywhere and the clean sun breaking through. In such a clearing atmosphere "American Negro Literature" became a distressing anachronism. This professor was none too happy even about the phrase.

No one challenged him that evening. How American Negro literature is taught is a matter of consequence. But it is not yet an issue of life or death. And over our coffee and beer and tobacco, at the fag end of a busy day, in the relaxed mood of the fabled frequenters of the Mermaid Tavern, we were really playing hopscotch with various subjects. Something intervened to turn our minds in a new direction before we had gotten our teeth into the matter of American Negro literature. Then, too, we had given witness to our fundamental sanity on the racial issue when we sat down. For our gathering was quietly, unselfconsciously interracial. And yet there *is* a case for American Negro literature.

That case starts where it is not invidious to say the Tennessee professor lost his way in some deductions of the third-order moment. With his deductions of the first- and second-order moment no one can find fault. Democracy does mean fair play all around. It ought to mean, therefore, the end of discrimination based on race in America. Segregation does constitute a form of such discrimination. Ergo, it should go. But that American Negro literature constitutes (or, rather, must constitute) a form of discrimination in the manner of segregation—ah, here it is that one may question the Tennessee professor's extrapolation of his own first principles.

The original cause of color caste in America is not for me to name. Probably it *was* economics, and if, in the familiar hypothesis, the cotton gin had never been invented, Negroes would have been freed long ago by a sort of natural process operating unobtrusively in the social order, so that today no more stigma would attach to Negro ancestry than, say, to Scotch-Irish. But the cotton gin was invented, or something did keep things going the wrong way for a long time. For generations, therefore, we have had in America the situation we have today—not just a system of color caste, but a tradition and a history of it as well. None of these three phenomena are quite the same thing. They are interdependent and often intermixed, intimately and inextricably so. But they are far from being altogether identical.

It is easier, for example, to change the system of color caste than to change the tradition. A law can do the first, as Negroes have learned from confronting the vagaries of Jim Crow throughout the South, and as some Supreme Court decisions have demonstrated in higher education. To change the tradition, however, requires that someone, either a teacher or a learner or both, unlearn something old and learn something new. This unlearning and learning anew is frequently so hard for people that a tradition does literally have to die out. The carriers of it in one form must literally, that is, perish before their version of the tradition can be supplanted. And, of course, to change the actual history of an institution like color caste is absolutely impossible. What has happened has happened, and there is an end to that.

Even when history is defined in its strict professional sense, as a collection of written records (incidentally, tradition has a habit of creeping into records, too), the only internal change that can occur in connection with it is subjective, not objective. Observers may change their way of evaluating a record. The record remains as it was. A collection of records may be enlarged by the addition of new records, so that the continuous record that all these records form may change. An observer's attitude toward an existing record may be affected thereby, but intrinsically history, whether as fact or record, does not change. It only grows. It is our knowledge of it, our feeling for it, that undergoes transubstantiation.

To say all this, however, is only to emphasize the pre-emptive character of tradition in color caste. Whether we put under glass the system or the history, we see always the tradition coalescing with the other two, and acting powerfully on them both, like Coleridge's shaping spirit of the imagination acting on the data of sense. At the same time, we cannot help but see again how very highly subjective tradition is as a living thing. It is as it is because people's inner thoughts are as they are. Not that the system and cold history do not exert their own pressures on our racial tradition. Segregation laws, for example, components of a system that they are, do help to make segregation seem "natural" wherever these laws exist. But still it is the tenacity and power of the tradition that do more to uphold the system than the system does to uphold the tradition. And what is true of the system of color caste is at least as true of its history.

Indeed, it may well be that the effect of the tradition on the history is more illustrative of the present imperial role of tradition in color caste than is the effect of tradition on the system. For instance, one of the most interested students of the Negro and the Old South was the late Ulrich B. Phillips. No one who has ever read Phillips can doubt that he was a person with a gift for writing history. He was well trained and he had studied his period with intensity and affection. Still it is instructive to examine this excerpt from the preface (dated 1919) to his *American Negro Slavery:*

My sojourn in a National Army Camp in the South while this book has been going through the press has reinforced my earlier conviction that Southern racial asperities are mainly superficial, and that the two great elements are fundamentally in accord. That the harmony is not a new thing is evinced by the very tone of the camp. The men of the two races are of course quartered separately; but it is a daily occurrence for white Georgian troops to go to the negro [sic][1] companies to seek out their accustomed friends and compare home news and experiences. The negroes themselves show the same easy-

1. My generation of Negroes used *sic* to voice our disapproval of whites like Phillip lowercasing *Negro* while they capitalized *Caucasian.* We were as sensitive to the lowercased *Negro* as we were to the pronunciation *Niggra.*

going, amiable, seriocomic obedience and the same personal attach-
ments to white men, as well as the same sturdy light-heartedness and
the same love of laughter and of rhythm, which distinguished their
forebears. The non-commissioned officers among them show a punc-
tilious pride of place which matches that of the plantation foremen of
old; and the white officers who succeed best in the command of these
companies reflect the planter's admixture of tact with firmness of
control, the planter's patience of instruction, and his crisp though
cordial reciprocation of sentiment.

What a revealing bit of expression this is! How subjective it
is! "Of course" the two races are quartered separately. Of
course, also, the white troops go down to the Negro companies.
Significantly, the Negro troops do not go "up" into the white
companies, and it seems safe to wager that Professor Phillips is
not at all disturbed by, if he is even aware of, the suspicion
that this one-sided freedom may not be a law of nature. The
highest rank that Negroes can attain in Professor Phillips'
army is that of noncommissioned officers. The *real* officers are
white. Moreover—one can read between Professor Phillips'
lines—they should be.

And why is all this true? The answer is plain. Professor
Phillips' reflexes about Negroes and the race question in
America were conditioned. He had preconceptions about
Negroes before he looked at them. His "easy-going, amiable,
seriocomically obedient" Negroes, lighthearted, laughter-
loving, and born with a racial genius for knowing their place,
are altogether too familiar. For decades they crooned along the
levees and picnicked in the cotton fields of the minstrel stage.
In the same gaslit era, they formed a staple dish of American
popular song. Likewise then they appeared, according to formula, not only in the cheap drama and fiction pitched down to
the entertainment level of the insensate crowd, but also, with
only a few exceptions here and there, in the most reputable of
serious literature. They were, that is, the effluvia of a tradition.
And if they shaped Professor Phillips' thinking in the preface
to one of his histories, nothing could be symbolically more apt.
That is where his steeping in the tradition belonged. It came

first; his historiographical self came after it and was considerably subject to it.

But Professor Phillips may serve to illustrate not only the power of a tradition, but also how that same tradition undergoes the process of change. In all fairness to him—and to ourselves—it is well to remember that a full generation has passed since the peak of his productive career, and two generations have passed since the attitudes that governed his basic reactions to people and situations hardened into their set form. A white boy growing up in America today will see few Aunt Jemimas and Gold Dust Twins; and, even as he does, they will tend to lose their conditioning power because of a spate of kindlier, truer representations of the Negro among the myriad impressions that flow into that boy day by day.

But social distance still wraps the Negro in some aura of mystery and dread for many white people. And the vestiges of any old tradition die hard. Above all this, of course, as we have seen, the great fact remains. A congeries of forces *is* working in its quiet tumult of mighty harmonies to bring about a change in the whole fabric of America's thinking on color caste. America's thinking on many problems, not originally problems of color caste, has achieved a sense of maturing responsibility that carries over into her thinking on color caste. Negroes themselves are changing. They dress more like other people now. They talk and act more like other people. They even look less "strange." America, too, is changing. The Civil War is fading now into a past of mist and softening haze. An urban culture that enjoys advantages of transportation and communication unknown to its predecessors has made village and farm an integral part of cosmopolis. And Americans, too, have changed. We are no longer so lonely, so uprooted, so desperate in our "search for a father" that we still savagely worship an in-group cult.

We may not see the benignities of our own age, for we are so close to ourselves. Our clear and present dangers block our field of vision. Moreover, elegy for the glories of the past is a curiously toothsome bonbon to the human spirit. Still we are, rank and file, a maturer nation in many ways than we ever were before. Certainly we are on matters of race. For a man of Professor Phillips' caliber to speak of Negroes in our own day as he seriously did in his would seem tragic and pitiful to most scholars of the 1950s. Scholarship can rightly say it is more objective now about Negroes than Phillips was. Scholarship can rightly say, that is, that for it a tradition has changed through rectification by fact. This is clearly the only process by which any tradition is changed for the better. And it is the process one possible extension of which — in its finest form — our Tennessee professor would eliminate if he ignored American Negro literature.

For, if any set of facts should serve properly to rectify our traditional concept of the American Negro, it should be evidence of what he actually is. That is exactly what American Negro literature is. Moreover, it is evidence not of what one or two Negroes are, but of what the majority of Negroes are and of what they have tended to be for some time. Today a good course in American Negro literature can provide a student of American life with a full and moving transcript of the Negro's own American consciousness. It can tell, as nothing else can, what Negroes really are. Sociology can not do the job so well. It is primarily an intellectual exercise, and it lacks the subjectivity of literature. Music is subjective enough, but it is *too* emotional, *too* subjective. It has no precise means of conveying its makers' intentions and meanings. And reading a book here, a poem there, by a Negro does not give quite the sense of historic sweep and continuity, the filling in of background, that a systematic knowledge of American Negro literature as a literature can supply.

As a matter of practical fact, the big thing wrong with integrating separate Negro works into general courses in American literature, as it would probably be done today, is that the men who might be called upon to do it would have no knowledge of American Negro literature as a whole. They would have been doing, in effect, nothing more than reading a book here or a poem there by a Negro. We do not ask for, or tolerate, analogous situations elsewhere. American Negro literature is not the only subdivision of American literature. Within this huge complex we have genre literatures like the novel or short story, period literatures like the American Renaissance, geographical literatures like the southern writers, and even, for our greatest writers, at least in terms of critical attention, compact little galaxies of literature grown up around individual stars. The compiler of a general treatment of American literature is not, of course, a specialist in all of these distinguishable, isolated areas. But he knows that there are specialists for each. Where he is not himself a specialist, he avails himself of the specialists' work and advice. Moreover, the mere presence of these specialists conditions his attitude. He is all the more careful of what he says, for he has been impressed with the significance of each of these subkingdoms as a subject for serious study.

Fair play—an accurate representation both of American literature as a complete record of American life and of American Negro literature properly interpreted within that record —can only come as a happy accident, without the service of the discipline implied by courses in American Negro literature. Magnanimous motives and sympathetic intentions are not sufficient in matters like these. Arduous training and the proper exploitation of its results are the least that will do. Otherwise, we shall continue to have works of Negro authorship selected for general treatment in courses of American literature and commented upon therein, in an ultimately haphazard fashion.

Even for the lay reader who only picks up a "Negro" book occasionally, American Negro literature may prove a boon. When this same reader picks up a work by Shakespeare or Melville, he may well have in the back of his mind certain ideas that help him to fathom the work. Certainly if he wants to understand Shakespeare or Melville better, there are available to him exegeses that permit him to put Shakespeare and Melville into larger contexts than his own experiences can supply. The systematic study of literature has occasioned these aids. The systematic study of American Negro literature is beginning to supply their like for Negro literature. One magazine especially, *Phylon*, at Atlanta University, is doing yeoman service in this field. Good men write for *Phylon*. They have been trained as have other American scholars and critics. They are becoming able now to transcend the desperate "political" impulse that once led virtually every Negro expatiating upon a piece of literature by another Negro to praise it, in the hope, apparently, that thereby more Negroes would be encouraged to write. The pressing problem of this moment is that whole books on American Negro literature are pitifully few. But the chances are that they are coming. For Negro literature today is what Crete was to scholarship when Sir Arthus Evans went to Knossus. It is a green pasture waiting for an eager flock to crop it; and American scholarly enterprise, unless artificially restrained, will not leave it forever so fresh.

A great American historian once pointed out that America was a land of frontiers. The physical frontiers have been engorged by our national appetite for a fuller life, one after another. They are gone now. The industrial frontiers are becoming increasingly harder to espy. But there still remain psychological frontiers to be penetrated and moulded in the image of the American dream. The sublimation of the old tradition of color caste is one of those psychological frontiers. And for the increasing number of Americans who, like our Tennessee professor, have been chagrined by the failure of democracy actually to work in its treatment of Negroes, meeting the challenge of that frontier is the categorical imperative. Far from saying that this is the time to abandon an American Negro literature, this is the time for us to tap its resources and to heap them up. Everything conspires, now, for this double action. The state of the literature permits it. It has come far enough at last to constitute the kind of record we need to prove that in truth American democracy has not failed where Negroes are concerned. And enlightened social engineering demands it. For enlightened social engineering warns us that, if color caste is really to be dissolved in America, it must be attacked in its heart. Its heart is a tradition, the tradition that renders palatable to too many Americans the perpetuation of color caste and even governs the manner in which the history of the race problem in America is to be presented.

In the most human terms, this is the case for Negro literature. And yet there is one word more, a word that should not be left unsaid. In a sense, the argument that courses in American Negro literature serve the ends of American democracy is an argument for expediency. Call the expedient noble, still it is a *quid pro quo*. People who work with literature, whether they write it or only interpret it, should be above mere expediency. Literature, said Matthew Arnold, is the criticism of *life*. It is, in other words, the relentless, insatiable, uncompromising search for truth. But this is a world of fluid definition, in which distinctions meet and merge even while they separate. What is most expedient for American democracy is also most true. It is true, for example, that Negro literature shows that for a long time a great schism has obtained in American life. Why should we, whatever our color, close our eyes to any evidences of that fact? It is not the only evil America has been great enough to overcome. Moreover, a careful reading of American Negro literature shows it improving steadily just because the social order from which it emanates is improving steadily in all its attitudes and gestures toward the makers of that literature and their kind. This is the truth, too—the sort of criticism of life that it is the highest office of literature to pursue indefatigably. It is also grounds for the best kind of hope to which men's finest expedients may be attached—hope founded, as the dedicated truth-seeker would wish it, on the solid facts of our earthly existence.

The Negro's
Image of His Universe
as Reflected
in His Fiction

THIS ESSAY *appeared first in the* CLA Journal *in 1960. I believe it was solicited, but I cannot recall, if it was solicited, the circumstances attendant upon its solicitation. It reached a wider audience through its appearance in Darwin Turner and Jean Bright (eds.),* Images of the Negro in America *and, later, in Abraham Chapman (ed.),* Black Voices.

⤢

Among the most notable effects of fiction is its capacity for producing within the limits of the illusion it creates a world which, even in the sense of the geographer and historian, can seem, almost literally, very true. There is undoubtedly a real England with a real past, a real present, and still, apparently, a quite respectable real future. But there is also, as many devoted readers know, an England of English fiction, a complete and separate world unlike any other fictional reality, built out of a set of distinctively English sensibilities recollected, if in tranquility, surely in some distinctively English versions of that often-admirable psychic state. Likewise, there is, within American literary tradition, a world of Negro fiction, within itself as singular a phenomenon as any other fictive world, and one as representative of a peculiar reaction to the objective facts of actual existence.

Three things seem, above all, to impart to this world of Negro fiction its distinctive character. One of these things is the physical shape that world assumes under the Negro writer's analytic eye. Another, somewhat harder to label, has to do with a power that seems to preside, like the ruling spirit in Thomas Hardy's *Wessex*, over all chains of consequence — thus controlling them with its own prescriptive intent and maintaining a mood, an atmospheric tone, that becomes thereby the prevailing temper of the whole universe. The third quality, hardest to name and hardest to describe precisely, is a matter of process, a sort of special law of the conservation of energy, ending in its own special pattern of circumscribed variability and its own special maintenance of a special *status quo*. Let us look, then, at each of these three things in order — at the way, to speak most simply, this universe looks, the way it feels, and at what may well be called its peculiar eschatology.

Surely the two most celebrated of Negro novels are Richard Wright's *Native Son* and Ralph Ellison's *Invisible Man*. In *Native Son*, the physical setting is Chicago. But only the most obtuse reader would fail to notice that the Chicago which establishes every point of reference in *Native Son* is the Chicago of the Negro ghetto. It is the only Chicago with which Bigger Thomas, the novel's black protagonist, can identify himself. Indeed, all creation, in the perspective of his well-conditioned reflexes, takes essential shape simply and clearly as ghetto and nonghetto — an extension of himself, as it were, into me and not me. And in this uncompromising dichotomy of his physical environment, to Bigger it is the ghetto, always the ghetto, that constitutes the prime reality. The nonghetto is the obligatory second term, the meaningful opposite without which the ghetto could not be seen for what it is. But as Chicago serves *Native Son*, so does New York serve *Invisible Man*. There are some minor differences. In *Invisible Man* the action does not open in New York, but it arrives there soon enough. And while its protagonist does see this metropolis outside of Harlem, as Bigger Thomas never quite sees Chicago beyond the South

Side, the fact remains that it is Harlem which pervades the book—just as it is Harlem, or its equivalent, which establishes the same radical division for the Invisible Man as Chicago's South Side does for Bigger Thomas, the division of the physical world in its totality into ghetto and nonghetto, that division which accounts alike for the Invisible Man's unique kind of invisibility and the Native Son's unique kind of nativeness.

That the two best known of Negro novels should put the emphasis they do upon the two largest Negro ghettos is an informative circumstance. Harlem and Chicago's South Side are ghettos easily allied with the classic pattern. Give each of them a wall, and they would then conform in every substantial respect to those famed quarters set aside for Jews in medieval towns from which ghettos have derived their name and definition. And it is only literally that Harlem and the South Side lack a wall. Likewise, it is only in the most literal terms that the campus on which the Invisible Man spends his most credulous and hopeful youth fails to be what it effectively is, merely another ghetto. Surely this campus differs much in outward show from the single squalid and sadly down-at-heel tenement room into which Bigger, his brother, his mother, and his sister compress all the activities of their life as a domestic household. It has green lawns, clean buildings, a quiet bourgeois atmosphere, and, when the moonlight broods upon its broad expanse, the sort of beauty which Matthew Arnold noted in his Oxford of the dreaming spires. Nevertheless, Mr. Norton, the white trustee, comes into it as a visitor from an altogether alien world. Thus would he have entered Harlem. Thus, too, would he have come into the Negro quarter of any small town, be it in the Kansas of Langston Hughes's *Not Without Laughter* or the Georgia of John Oliver Killens' *Youngblood*. And thus, too, would he have entered the agrarian South of Negro peasants such as George Wylie Henderson's *Jule* or *Ollie Miss*. For what has happened in virtually every piece of Negro fiction brooks but one interpretation, whether its creator was working as a conscious artist or whether his divided landscape comes unwittingly into focus under his spontaneous hand. All Negro fiction tends to conceive of its physical world as a sharp dichotomy, with the ghetto as its central figure and its symbolic truth—and with all else comprising a nonghetto, which throws into high relief the ghetto itself as the fundamental fact of life for Negroes as a group.

This has been consistently the case with fiction by Negro authors since the earliest novel of Negro authorship, William Wells Brown's *Clotel,* itself a travelogue through much of the extensive ghetto formed by the *mise en scene* of American slavery. A few exceptions to this general condition do exist. I instance as examples of such exceptions Charles W. Chesnutt's short story, "Baxter's Procrustes," basically a *jeu d'esprit,* and Ann Petry's novel, *Country Place,* one of the several sustained fictions of Negro authorship in which a Negro writer has attempted to write of the predominantly white world as a white person would. But I should not want to concede as exceptions of significant worth such novels about white life as Frank Yerby's sensational fantasies, which make no pretense at seriousness, nor even similarly oriented works like Willard Motley's *Knock on Any Door,* about which one can hardly escape the conclusion voiced recently by Robert Bone—that it is a lesser *Native Son* masquerading as a treatment of Skid Row. Moreover, so firmly holds this rule of the ghetto over the landscape of Negro fiction that one may be sure that exceptions to it *are* exceptions. And like all true exceptions, they disprove no generalizations; they only prove the rule.

But so much, now, for this universe as physical shape. Let us consider briefly its special feel.

There is a word in our language, *irony,* which a strong tradition in American life has been at great pains never to associate with the Negro character. Negroes, avers this strong tradition, are comic, primitive, savage in ways sometimes gay, sometimes brutal, but never so mature, so complex, so civilized as to be capable of making the subtle distinctions required of a practitioner of irony. For *irony* derives from classical Greek, the language of a people themselves mature, complex, and highly civilized—a people, that is, separated by many generations of superior culture from the barbaric innocence and crudity of the Negro collective consciousness. Moreover, the first great ironist of historic note was Socrates, thinker par excellence and master of dialectic. Only the wildest heresy would link him with the typical representative of anything having to do with Negroes.

It must be admitted that irony could hardly consort with children or with minstrel men. It requires a certain refinement of perception. It depends upon that nice derangement of affairs in which an outcome is incongruous with an expectation. In addition, within some observer it must produce a very special kind of emotional discord. It must cause that observer, at one and the same time, pleasure and pain. He must want, simultaneously, to laugh and cry. In art, of course, form is a necessary adjunct, and students of irony have noted that, once given the proper ironic incongruity, that incongruity may express itself in three ways. It may be irony of speech, when what is said carries a meaning incongruous with its meaning on first examination, the incongruity producing the proper emotional discord. It may be irony of character, when what a person actually is turns out to be incongruous with what he seems to be, again with the proper emotional effect. (Here, of course, Socrates belongs—who seemed so stupid and was so wise; and here, too, belong all dissemblers of his ilk, including a long line of Uncle Toms.) For ironic dissimulation, the concealing of superior knowledge on the part of the ironist—a special skill of Socrateses as of Uncle Toms—is inseparable from irony of character. Finally, there may be an irony of events, when a train of events ends with an outcome incongruous with the expectation, still, of course, with the attendant proper emotional effect of conjunctive pain and laughter in the observer.

To think of some of the titles of Negro novels, especially with the contents of those novels clearly in mind, is at once to begin to suspect, no matter how subtle an ironist is supposed to be, that irony may play a large role in the universe of Negro fiction. *Native Son* is certainly an irony of speech, in view of the conditions which lawyer Max contends made Bigger Thomas the logical outcome, the true son, of his environment; and so is *One Way to Heaven*, for where does Sam Lucas go and how does he get there? So, also, are *Last of the Conquerors*, with its double, if not triple, puns on *Last* and *Conquerors; The Blacker the Berry*, whose Emmy Lou does not find the juice of life sweet in any regard; *Comedy, American Style; If He Hollers, Let Him Go; Tambourines to Glory; The Walls of Jericho*, which have yet to tumble; *God Sends Sunday; The Living Is Easy;* even *The Autobiography of an Ex-Coloured Man*. But it is only when one begins to probe Negro fiction beyond its titles that one truly initiates himself into the great extent to which the presiding genius in the universe of Negro fiction is the ogre of an irony—or, to be more specific, the ogre of one particular irony—so ubiquitous in the Negro world that it seems to be every Negro's *vade mecum* and so gross in its proportions that, in strong contradiction to the inherent logic of ironic perception, no exquisiteness of sensibility is required to feel the dry mock of its incongruity. This particular irony is, of course, bound up with American color caste. All over America life is lived, officially and otherwise, only in the name of democracy. It is that way now. It has been that way since there was an America, for the Declaration of Independence, which proclaimed American nationhood, also proclaimed American democracy. But all over America how different from the name of democracy are the practices of color caste! How incongruous with an expectation is this ironic outcome!

And so, well nigh as omnipresent in the world of Negro fiction as the figure of the ghetto is the irony of color caste. Not to see exactly this one irony in Negro fiction is really not to see what is present there at all. But to see this irony is to become one with the Negro writer and to prove upon one's emotional pulse the Negro writer's world exactly in the manner of the Negro writer himself. Thus, in Ann Petry's *The Street*, the protagonist, Lutie Johnson, has a special reaction to a main street in one of those Connecticut towns where the right men in gray flannel suits live with their wives, their relatives and in-laws, their pets, and their often secretly bitter domestics, of whom Lutie for a time was one. That Connecticut street is to Lutie an all-too-tangible reminder of a condition she pines to attain, but from which she is forever barred. It is the suppressed term of an irony given the substance of an objective correlative. Against that street, that objective correlative, Lutie may later put, in her own mind, the street on which she comes to live in Harlem with her son and only child, Bub. Where the Connecticut street is clean, the Harlem street—*the* street, incidentally, of the novel's title—is foul. Where the Connecticut street is open and free and radiant to Lutie's inner eye, the Harlem street is hemmed in and furtive and drab in its meannesses and its makeshifts. Where the Connecticut street is a bourgeois heaven, the Harlem street is a bourgeois hell. And to make especially this latter contrast, the most important of them all, as forcefully as it can be made, Ann Petry has done all she can to project an image of Lutie Johnson's psychology as that of an unabashed and uncritical bourgeois. Lutie is one of the faithful. She had bargained her soul on getting ahead. Does she not take a course at night, and then an examination, to get the job which frees her from servitude in the white man's household? She is strong—Mrs. Petry provides her with a magnificent physique—young, intelligent, determined, and willing to work hard in the best tradition of Alexander Hamilton, Stephen Girard, John D. Rockefeller, and General Motors. Not one tiniest trace of skepticism corrupts her orthodoxy. Nothing mars the wholeness of her devotion. Karl Marx would be unthinkable for her, Thorstein Veblen, a tiresome dilettante. And certainly she would have only bewildered contempt for the kind of rebellion against Philistia with which the modern artist has assaulted Mrs. Grundy since the earliest days of modern art's many isms.

By all odds the outcome of Lutie's expectations should be the street in the Connecticut town. But the irony of color caste makes it the street in the Harlem ghetto, directly the descendant of the row of slave cabins in the antebellum plantation for which the idiom of the slave South often used the generic name, "the street." As it is with *The Street*, so is it with the overwhelming bulk of Negro fiction. The scene is not always Harlem. The characters are not always as naively trustful of the democratic dream as Lutie Johnson. But the irony is virtually always present, changing its incidental details, never changing its fundamental terms — a distinctive component of the universe of Negro fiction and a component without which the universe would be very materially altered in significance and value.

But now I want to proceed to the third, and final, major feature I have chosen to cite in the universe of Negro fiction. About this feature one may not, because of its very nature, speak as categorically as one may about the other two. And yet it is, I am convinced, a feature that should not be ignored.

All universes subject to human observation seem to operate according to some principle that determines the character of the universe. Conceivably the principle may actually be more subjective than it is anything else. Nevertheless the men who inhabit the universe believe in its reality, and tend to accommodate their actions and their thoughts to that belief. For example, to the Vikings whose world appears in the Norse sagas the great principle that governed process in the universe was conflict. The end of all things was to come in a battle between the Frost Giants and the Gods, and the passport to Valhalla was death in combat. Thus the world of Viking culture flames with the burnings of halls and clangs with the weapons of warriors feuding in obedience to custom. On the other hand, the world of medieval Christendom, for all of Saint Augustine's *City of God*, is relatively tensionless. It is basically a holding action, the keeping in place of a great chain of being proceeding downward from God, the Unmoved Mover, through the lowest realm of an hierarchical order and back again to its source, a closed circuit in which the decisive process is not change, but maintenance of the established pattern.

In the American tradition, however, change has been the historic process. This nation was not born until after the idea of progress, no sop to the Cerberus of any *ancien regime.* If physiocratic thought with its Newtonian science got into this nation's constitution, at least by the age of Jackson this nation's politics, in theory and practice, reflected also the Godwinian optimism which assumed that the Watchmaker Universe was wound up to bring on, be it ever so gradually, the sometime utopia of the perfectability of man. For generations of American life, what this benevolent philosophy of cosmic process hypostasized, the moving frontier, unfolding the bounty of a rich continent, tended to confirm. To a New England Brahman or to one of Edith Wharton's old New Yorkers, that frontier may not have been an unmixed blessing. But to humbler folk, until the last homestead vanished and the great corporations captured the national economy, it must have seemed a welcome evidence that opportunity, all anyone needed in America to improve himself, was built into the grand design. Even a fierce old aristocrat like James Fenimore Cooper, romancing the brief past that America had accumulated in his, to our nation, youthful day, cannot fail to produce in his fiction an America in which change plays an important role. Or even more curiously, a Willa Cather, intoning elegies for that golden time which she always located in the American past, could not have lamented as she did had she not premised as the indispensable background for her sweet moan a changing social order.

But the world of Negro fiction is as static as the world of the medieval synthesis. It is a world in which the distinctive cosmic process is not change, but a holding action. In the typical Negro novel, after all the sound and fury dies, one finds things substantially as they were when the commotion began. At the end of *Native Son* the world of Bigger Thomas does not differ from the one he has always known. It was, and

is, a world in which, season in and season out, the elemental
process is a holding action, the maintenance of a continuing,
unaffected relationship of caste to caste in the American pattern of color caste. We know, at the end, that Bigger has made
an effort to redefine his relationship with the world. We know
that he has not succeeded in meaningful terms. But we know
also that his failure does not involve the reconciliation of
variables, except as he has undergone an intensification of his
own ability to perceive. And in *Invisible Man,* the world with
which we deal is static. When the Invisible Man keeps asking
himself his question about Tod Clifton—keeps wanting to
know, that is, why Clifton has dropped out of history—the
language deceives no one. There is no history in *Invisible Man*
in the sense that history is change. All that Tod Clifton has
dropped out of is a picture, not a process, at least not a process
rendered operational by its function as change. I should say
offhand that among major pieces of Negro fiction, only in
Langston Hughes's *Not Without Laughter* and John Oliver
Killens' *Youngblood* is the phenomenon of change to be dis-
cerned in the constitution of the fictional universe. To an overwhelming degree the universe of Negro fiction is panoramic,
not dramatic. It is a still picture, the unchanging backdrop
against which actors are paraded to show how fixed is a setting
which should be, but has not been, altered in its essential features. It is, in short, the limited universe of a literature of protest, a universe that, with its quality of *stasis,* can well be seen
as the same universe which Negroes see, but only from two
different angles, when they see first in it either the ghetto or
the irony of color caste.

And now let me finish off this brief excursion into the world
of Negro fiction with a final observation. It seems to me that
few, if any, literary universes are as impoverished as is the universe of Negro fiction. I have spoken of some things that can
be found there. Of greater moment, conceivably, are the things
that cannot be found there. In a famous passage in his *Haw-
thorne,* Henry James once bemoaned the things America

lacked. Much more can a sympathetic critic bemoan the absence of a plethora of things devoutly to be desired in the world of Negro fiction. And of even greater moment, it may well be, is the fact that everything in this universe of Negro fiction seems too easily convertible into one primal substance. To look for any length of time at this world is to see the ghetto melt into the irony of color caste, the irony of color caste melt into the holding action that is this universe's law of *stasis*, this holding action melt into the ghetto, and so on until all is one and one is all. But should universes be so monolithic? Not, I think, even when they are fictional. There must be much about the universe, even about the Negro universe which is their special care, that Negroes have not said in their fiction. Who can say, who looks soberly at what has been done, that Othello's occupation is anything but far from being gone?

Richard Wright:
Black Boy from
America's Black Belt
and Urban Ghettos

SHORTLY *before Richard Wright's untimely death, I began to think of, and work upon, largely as the result of urging from a publisher, a book-length study of this migrant from Mississippi who had done so well outside of Mississippi. It seemed to me, however, as if everything happened to impede my progress on the book which is still in a sort of midpassage between its conception and its final execution.*

In a memorial issue for Wright of the CLA Journal *the part of my study which dealt with Wright's life was published. Indeed, my old friend, the editor of the* Journal, *Therman O'Daniel, accorded it the honor of leading off the special issue, not illogically when the content of this portion of my study is considered.*

I have another name for this portion of the study—a name shorter and more pungent. Someday I hope to use that name in the study, and also to apply it to the study as a whole.

⋈

Richard Wright was born in Mississippi, in a rural area some twenty-five miles from the town of Natchez, on September 4, 1908. His father, whose given name was Nathan, has been variously described as a sharecropper and a mill worker. This is a distinction very much without a difference. For, wherever he went, whatever he did, essentially Nathan Wright was always and utterly a sharecropper. Essentially, moreover, any mill in which he labored would have been like him, as integral a part of the South's agrarian economy as a field of cotton or as any, and all, of the highly regional towns in Arkansas and Mississippi where his son, in an important adjunct of that son's progress toward a precocious manhood, acquired an intimate clinical knowledge of the fundamental nature of color caste in America.

Wright's father apparently was one of those Negroes about whose ethnic identity there can be little question. His skin was rather dark. He was also an absolute illiterate, never having set foot inside a schoolroom in his entire life. In formal training, then, as well as in complexion, he differed from the young woman christened Ellen Wilson whom he took in marriage. She was, Edwin Embree tells us, "light brown, good looking, [and] possessed of a few years of book learning."[1] The relative lightness of her skin is understandable. She had a mother who was constantly being mistaken for white, as well as other Negro relatives equally lacking in discernible evidences of their Negro blood. Her good looks may have borrowed something from an Indian, added to a white and Negro, ancestry. Her son, our Wright, was to be "good looking," too, with a cast of feature in which, as in his genealogy, Caucasian, Mongol, and African would seem to blend, and with a skin more brown than black.

Any crossings of racial strains in Wright's genealogy, however, were not to be duplicated in his early experience of life. That was to be, until his most impressionable years were quite over, exclusively American Negro. It would seem, indeed, almost as if some tutelary spirit were presiding over his destiny, charged with strict obedience to an injunction from the Fates: "This boy must learn, comprehensively and powerfully, exactly what it means to be a Negro. Not a Negro of the black bourgeoisie who might go to Fisk (or even to an eastern college) and join a Negro college fraternity, and perhaps journey every August to the Negro tennis 'nationals' and every Christ-

---

1. Edwin Embree, *13 Against the Odds* (New York, 1944), 26. "Good looking," it should be remembered, in American parlance almost invariably connotes "good" according to an Aryan standard of right and wrong in personal appearance.

mas holiday with his wife to her Negro sorority convention. No! This boy must be Negro as the masses of Negroes have been Negro. He must know at firsthand their peasantry in the South, so pastoral in fable, so bitter in fact, their groping folk exoduses to the North and West, the grubbiness of their existence in the ghettos of America's greatest cities above the Mason-Dixon Line. He must emanate directly from the anonymous black throng, and what that throng has been forced to do, he must be forced to do also."

And so Wright's personal history does begin, as according to such an injunction it should, deep within the world of the folk Negro in the cotton-growing Delta, the world of all American worlds, when Wright was born, closest in form and substance to the plantation world of the antebellum South. Somewhere in the atavistic Delta countryside, probably in more than one sharecropper's cabin—for sharecroppers have compulsively tended toward nomadism in their search for the ideal tenancy—Wright must have spent his very earliest years. His earliest published recollections, however, in *Black Boy,* his own account of his youth, place his family in Natchez. Wright then was four years old, with a brother, the only brother or sister Wright ever mentions, a year younger than himself. One can well imagine, at this still probationary stage in their lives, what must almost surely have been his parents' shared sentiments. They were young, and youth is notoriously buoyant. Undoubtedly they must have cherished some of those sanguine dreams of making things better for their children which tend to unite parents of every moment and milieu. And so these parents gathered their children and themselves and went up the big river (did they think of their many slave forebears who had come down the same river?) to mount as it were, an assault on Memphis. They found, in Memphis, living quarters in a one-story brick tenement. The father found a job, as a night porter in a Beale Street drugstore. But he found also, and all too soon, a temptress like the Circes of scriptural Babylon, another woman, unattached, who quickly blotted from his

mind whatever conventional plans he may have brought with
him to Memphis. Before Wright was old enough to go to school,
this father had completely forsaken the wife and the two small
sons for whose presence in alien territory he was largely ac-
countable. He left them just as they were in the one-story brick
tenement. His person and all of his support he transferred to
the other woman.

The three Wrights thus marooned were in parlous condition. There were whole days after the father's departure
when they ate nothing simply because they had no money with
which to purchase food. Wright's mother, on occasion, had
taught school in the Delta. But Memphis was not the Delta and
her formal training, after all, was meager by any standards.
She took, therefore, the first job she could obtain, as a cook,
while she dispatched to her relatives urgent appeals for funds
that would enable her, with her sons, to retreat from Memphis.
At the same time she did not neglect her sons' claims upon
their father's interest. She hauled the father into court on a
petition for aid for these sons. A judge, who may have been
more percipient than the mother in her bitterness supposed,
accepted the father's stubborn avowal that he was doing all
he could. She did not rest, however, with this rebuff from the
law. Over Richard's strenuous objections she persuaded him
to accompany her on an expedition which, virtual infant that
he still was, yet seemed to him both shameful and futile. The
two confronted her husband in the room he was occupying
with the woman who had replaced her. Wright recreated the
encounter in *Black Boy*, referring there to his father's mistress
as the "strange woman." Wright's mother put her pride aside
to beg her husband for money—not, she was careful to point
out, to relieve her own distress, but to pay for the transportation of their two boys to a sister of hers in Arkansas. The father
laughed in her face as he rejected her plea. And the "strange
woman," true to her role, witting or not, of the ruthless siren
from secular Negro folk song, threw her brazen arms posses-
sively around the father's neck.

Wright's mother was hardly more successful with Memphis than she was with her husband. She had trouble keeping a job, for she was already beginning to show a disposition toward invalidism. She found it difficult also, on the low-paying jobs that were the only means of gainful employment available to her, to provide even the mere creature necessities and the proper supervision for her boys. For a time, indeed, while he was barely six, Wright became a drunkard, enticed into daily tipsiness by the Negro clientele of a nearby saloon for their own ribald sport. Wright's mother put a stop to this drunkenness by placing Wright, during the hours of the day while she was away at work, under the strict surveillance of an older woman who lived nearby. Yet Wright's mother still had the problem of a woefully insufficient income. She could not make ends meet. To avoid the rent she could not pay eventually, she put her two sons in an orphanage. But it was an orphanage which traduced every principle of Good Samaritanism. Its queasy food was doled out in starvation rations. The unfortunate inmates did little except pull grass, a curious chore they were encouraged to perform because the orphanage could not afford to pay for the mowing of its lawns. To cap everything for Wright, the spinster in charge, whose very appearance and manner set Wright's teeth on edge, doted heavily on him and wanted to adopt him. Small wonder that Wright ran away from this Dickensian horror, albeit not for long. His deliverance came through his mother's relatives. They sent her, at last, the money to withdraw, with her sons, to that sister of hers in Arkansas.

The Wrights' trip to Arkansas was preceded by a stop in Jackson. The parents of Wright's mother lived there then, in a fairly large house of two stories given to them by one of their sons. If any dwelling in which Wright lived until he became a man could be called his home—and none could—this was to be it. In this dwelling he was to spend six years, his last six years of dependence, or semidependence, on anyone other than himself. But first he was taken to Arkansas, where he

was to stay for four years, interrupted only by one brief return
to Jackson. His mother's sister in Arkansas had married
prosperously. Her husband owned a thriving saloon in Elaine.
The three Wrights were comfortable with him and well fed.
But he was shot to death not long after the Wrights joined
his household, Wright avers by whites who coveted the business he would not relinquish; and his wife and the three
Wrights, in dread of what might happen further, fled Elaine,
under cover of the dark, for West Helena, another Arkansas
town not far away. The four fugitives stayed in West Helena
for a time, went back to Jackson, then retraced their steps to
West Helena. The two women took menial jobs. Wright was
even able to attend school with some regularity. He was in
school in West Helena when the Armistice of 1918 was announced. But another night of terror came. When it passed,
Wright's aunt was gone, vanished like a wraith along a trail
that led into the fabled North, with a companion, only a vague
figure to Wright, the man who had attached himself to her in
West Helena. Behind them the escapees left a darksome
shadow of something sinister and violent, perhaps dangerously
interracial, that Wright never penetrated. In West Helena it
now became as it had once been in Memphis. Wright's mother,
left alone, found herself more than hard-put to try to provide
for herself and her two sons. Then came a morning of another
kind of terror. Wright's brother shook Wright out of his sleep.
The younger lad was frightened and frustrated, tremulous,
and bewildered. He wanted Wright to look at their mother.
Wright did, and called the neighbors, who summoned a doctor.
The mother was paralyzed. Now the two boys, neither yet in
his teens, were effectively alone. Within days they were back
in Jackson with a mother who would never be able to fend for
herself, or for them, again.

In Jackson new dispensations were arranged. Wright's
brother was sent north to rejoin the aunt with whom the
Wrights had lived in Arkansas. Wright was given a choice of
residence with any of his other maternal aunts and uncles.

He elected the uncle at Greenwood, Mississippi, nearest to his mother in Jackson. But he could not endure life with this uncle and the uncle's wife, kind though the couple tried their best to be. Soon Wright entrained once more for Jackson. He was returning to the house where his afflicted mother at least could give him some feeling of belonging.

The house in Jackson was dominated by his grandmother, a matriarch whose husband's only interest was his fantastic feud with Washington over a Civil War pension his right to which he had vainly tried for half a century to establish. The matriarch herself was a Seventh Day Adventist and like a member of a persecuted sect in the intensity of her zeal for the true faith. Her house was grim with the grimness of a genteel, hopeless poverty. But it was even grimmer with the requirements of the matriarch's devotional austerities. Worse yet, protest as Wright would, he was forced into attendance at a Negro Seventh Day Adventist school in Jackson. Wright did not like the school. He vastly preferred the competitive environment of public education. He liked even less the teaching. This emanated from the sole instructor, a young aunt of Wright's, domiciled under the same roof with him, unsure of herself in her first professional assignment, and cherishing for Wright a temperamental detestation, intensified and enlarged by their teacher-pupil relationship, which he heartily reciprocated. Wright knew he could not continue at this school. Only when he threatened almost hysterically to leave his family altogether was he able, however, to wring from his grandmother permission to transfer from Seventh Day Adventist tutelage to the public schools. In Memphis he had had some months of primary training. He had spent perhaps more than a year all told in school in West Helena. He did not finish a term in Greenwood. His one consecutive experience of formal education that lasted long enough to be considerable came now, in Jackson from 1921 to 1925. When, in June of the latter year, he had gone as far as he could go in the schools of Jackson and had finished their highest grade—a ninth grade which he noted constituted a review of the eighth — his formal education was completed.

Jackson offered Wright no future he could accept with equanimity. He was a Negro in the South. He was trained to do nothing of the slightest consequence. Besides — and here was for him the greater rub — since he had first had whispered to him when he was eight or nine, by a girl school-teacher boarding at his grandmother's, the story of Bluebeard, there had been, firm and unshakable in his will, the resolution to become a writer. Indeed he had already had a story published in the Jackson Negro weekly newspaper, a tale called "The Voodoo of Hell's Half-Acres," and had been rebuked by his grandmother for the language of the title as well as for the added sinfulness of telling, for any reason whatever, anything but the "truth." And still, he never seems to have thought seriously of any permanent vocation other than writing. Until, however, he could write, he had to live. He tried his hand at some of the "Negro" jobs available to him in Jackson. Not only were they leading him nowhere, he sensed, too, a danger in them. He sensed that, in his manner of performing the servile tasks associated with them, he was not acting "right." He was not conducting himself as a Negro should. An opportunity came for him to make a windfall in a petty swindle. He seized it, and supplemented his ill-gotten gains with the proceeds from his one excursion into burglary.

Now through with crime for the rest of his days, and saying farewell only to his mother, he stealthily quitted Jackson in the autumn of 1925 for Memphis. In Memphis for two years he worked at another, but better, Negro job with a large optical firm. His best job in Jackson had been also with an optical firm. He managed to reunite with himself his mother and his brother as well as his aunt from his Arkansas days, who had lost, somewhere along her way, the vaguely figured companion with whom she had departed from West Helena. He saved some money. He began to read avidly on his own. He had access gratis to magazines and newspapers around the building in which he worked. Procuring books was not nearly so easy. He solved that problem with the help of a white employee of the optical firm. He would present himself at the public library with a list of books ostensibly from the employee, and with this employee's card, and thus acquire for his own use the loan of books he wanted to read. But, of course, Memphis was still not the environment for him. He broke the news one day, as diffidently as he could, to his employers at the optical firm that he was leaving, since he was in the position of being "forced" to "accompany" his aunt and his paralyzed mother to Chicago. He had arrived at the end of a first stage in his own life. Behind him was an impressionable youth spent in an urgent roving commission that had immersed him in the folk life of the American Negro at its very base, while it also denied him any semblance of a normal childhood, a protected environment, and any convenient fantasies about the nature of social truth. Ahead of him, he hoped, would be a chance to learn to write.

Chicago by 1927 may have come to constitute the ideal spot for a Negro writer who wanted thoroughly and reliably to understand the Negro as an American phenomenon. It is even doubtful whether Harlem, always the largest and greatest, and the best known, of American Negro ghettos,[2] was truly quite as representative of American Negro life between the two world wars as the Black Belt of the South Side. For Harlem evinced, here and there in what it was able to compound with, a strangeness, an easygoing toleration of cosmopolitanism, that was not always American. And the Negro is the most wistfully American of all Americans. He wants to be accepted, on American terms by American people. From Harlem, for example, in the twenties a Negro of very sable hue, one Marcus Garvey, intoned his dream of black nationalism, a united Africa, every inch of it governed by black men in the interest of, and with the support, of black people everywhere. "Up, you mighty race," he exhorted. And the black masses of America did respond to

2. And, all through the twenties virtually, in ferment with the Harlem, or Negro, Renaissance.

his exhortation. But it is instructive to examine dispassionately, indeed cynically, the nature of their response. They did not go to Africa. They never have, in sizable numbers to stay, under any persuasion. They long ago learned to want, with the rest of immigrant America, the best of two worlds, a respectable past in some distant overseas and a respectable present, or the reasonable hope of it, among their American neighbors.

Provisional Orders of the Black Legion, provisional duchies in Kenya and Uganda as hereditary rights, possessed a psychological value, on this side of the Atlantic, for Negroes who were bowed down beneath the weight of honorific European pasts to which they could lay no claim. The Black Belt of Chicago in the twenties, therefore, a teeming wedge within Chicago's South Side, extending seven miles south from Chicago's Loop, almost uniformly more than a mile wide, and growing like any good American boom town in everything except, significantly, its geographical boundaries — its 44,000 Negro inhabitants in 1910 having become 109,000 in 1920 and moving on to become the 237,000 of 1930 — did not attract its large inpouring of Negroes from the South [3] because of any thirst those Negroes had for foreign conquest or pan-Africanism. Chicago in the twenties had its own exhorter to black America. He was as sable of hue as Marcus Garvey. But Garvey was from Jamaica in the British West Indies. The mind of the American Negro was never quite in fact an open book to him.

Robert S. Abbott, on the other hand, was, like most of Chicago's Negroes, from the American South — in his own case from Georgia. He had made his way to the Illinois eldorado through the classrooms of Hampton Institute, where he acquired a mastery of printing. On the South Side, in the early 1900s, he had started a weekly newspaper, the Chicago *Defender*, which by the 1920s called itself the "World's Greatest

---

3. As late as the early 1940s St. Clair Drake and Horace Cayton in their careful study of the Negro in Chicago, *Black Metropolis* (New York, 1945), were to find (see p. 99) that over eighty out of every one hundred "Chicago" Negroes had been born in the South.

Weekly" and which did carry its message by then, in some form or other, into virtually every nook and cranny of Negro America. The "Up, you mighty race" Abbott advocated was Negro migration from the South, and when he stood on his Mount Pisgah and crooned down to the Negro masses his telescopic view of the promised land that Negroes were to seek, one had only to eliminate Abbott's references to race to hear in accents pure the booster's choice of George F. Babbitt. Abbott came, indeed, at about the very time that Wright was settling in Chicago, to the campus of a Negro university and there told the undergraduates, in convocation assembled, but still agape from the epiphanic vision of Abbott's emergence from the plush recesses of a chauffeur-driven Rolls Royce, that in Chicago his money was enabling him to pass for white. He spoke not gloatingly, but as an Old Testament prophet dutifully expounding holy writ. His audience listened in a hush of unfeigned reverence.[4] For his audience knew of Jesse Binga, the Pullman porter who became president of one of Chicago's two Negro banks, of Oscar DePriest, the Negro who was to go to Congress from the South Side in 1928, of Daniel Hale Williams, the Chicago Negro surgeon who had operated on the human heart. With Abbott, indeed, this audience shared a black nationalism that began and ended only as a protest against the exclusion of the Negro from full participation in American life as the most conformist of Americans would have defined that life in the era of Harding and Coolidge. Abbott typified for this audience, therefore, what it truly dreamed of, or almost so. For, truth to tell, Abbott himself died without actually ever "passing for white." Abbott belonged, really, only to a black bourgeoisie. And so, for that matter, did Binga and DePriest and Dr. Williams. What Abbott did have was a certain ease in the externalia of affluence. He did not have the psychological gratifications or the communal privileges of the elect. And still he, and his kind, were relatively fortunate. The

4. The campus was that of Wilberforce University in southern Ohio. The date is uncertain. I was a contributor to the reverent hush.

vast bulk of Negroes in America in the twenties belonged to no kind of bourgeoisie. If they were not peasants on the land they were members of an urban proletariat.[5]

The migrant Wright in 1927, a nineteen-year-old boy with no well-placed friends on the South Side, or anywhere else in Chicago, and no acquisitions in training or property that would invest him with economic or social power, had to become an addition to black Chicago's urban proletariat. Ten years of living with Chicago Negroes in the mass — Wright was to leave for New York in 1937 — were to make him privy to the intimate condition of the black Chicagoan as nineteen years of residence in the upper Mississippi Delta and its hinterland had made him privy to the intimate condition of the southern Negro in that Negro's native habitat. He did not merely view the anonymous Negro masses of Chicago with a novelist's eye for material or a scientist's trained detachment. He existed for years as one of them. It may be hard to define the typical American Negro. It would certainly be impossible to define him, particularly as he was before the 1950s, without taking into account both the Negro of the agrarian and the small-town South and his often pathetically impotent cousin in the industrial North. For twenty-nine years of his life Wright never passed through a whole day without rubbing a fraternal shoulder with one, or both, of these Negroes.

His first job in Chicago was as a porter in a white delicatessen. He found this job by the simple expedient of getting on a streetcar, riding on it until he was out of the Black Belt, dismounting from his conveyance, and then trudging the cold winter streets until he saw a sign announcing that a porter was wanted. His next job was as a dishwasher in a white restaurant. He had taken, while he was portering, the civil service examina-

5. On the basis of the occupational distribution of Negroes, E. Franklin Frazier stipulates that in the four northern cities containing, in 1940, Negro communities numbering 100,000 or more, a bourgeoisie element constituted a little more than a fifth of the total Negro population. See Frazier, *Black Bourgeoisie* (Glenco, Ill., 1957), 46–47. Chicago was, of course, among those four cities. A Negro bourgeoisie was certainly proportionately no greater in the 1920s than in the 1940s.

tion for the Chicago Postal Service. In 1929 he received a substitute clerkship in the Chicago Post Office. He tells of remembering the cries of newsboys hawking the story of the stock market crash to the Chicagoans past whom he was proceeding as he savored the contents of the letter that had brought him notice of his appointment. Work in the post office not only relieved him of menial labor; it gave him time and left him energy for reading and practice at writing. But the cries of the newsboys, had he but known it, had been at least as much an omen for his life in Chicago as his letter. The Great Depression came and deepened. Through another examination he had raised his postal rating, but the mails were feeling the effects of the times. He was laid off at the post office, and again looking for any job he could find. A stint of duty as agent for various Negro insurance firms improved his knowledge of the Black Belt, but did not solve his problem of caring for the household for which he considered himself responsible. He went on relief and for a while swept streets as a relief worker at thirteen dollars a week. But after the relief authorities placed him as a worker at the South Side Boys' Club—with its provision of close, continuous scrutiny of young Negroes from the Black Belt streets, a job peculiarly appropriate for the writing he was now soon to accomplish—the tasks he performed for subsistence moved ever closer to the things he wanted to do as a matter of self-expression. He was transferred from the boys' club to an assignment as publicity agent for the Federal Negro Theater. Then, still with WPA (Works Progress Administration), he was transferred, again as publicity agent, to a white federal experimental theater. Finally he came, still through the ranks of WPA, to the Federal Writers' Project, with which he became an acting supervisor of essays before he left Chicago.

So his life went, through much of the 1930s. And yet his life was much more vivid, much fuller of the play of incident, once incident is conceived as happenings in an inner as well as an outer world, than any running account of it can suggest. For one thing he was reading, making himself into something of an intellectual, and talking, no longer to the unread, but to many keen youngsters like himself—like him in their keenness, at least; mostly they were white—for whom the life of the mind carried far beyond the Philistias of an Abbott or a Garvey. For another thing, he was trying his hand at writing, practicing at learning a craft too exacting for dilettantes and amateurs, devoting long hours to the business of constructing sentences —a mystery he found that exposed itself only to relentless pursuit—and charging himself for the big job of writing a novel, in the spirit, it would seem, of Keats as Keats approached the parallel necessity, for him, of doing the long poem *Endymion.* And for a final thing Wright had encountered communism, an experience by no means unusual for the intellectually curious during the era of the Great Depression.

Wright has had his say about his bout with communism in the essay he contributed to the symposium, *The God that Failed.* He made his acquaintance with it through the intermediation of the Chicago John Reed Club, an organization of left-wing writers and painters to which he was attracted by the recommendation of a young Jewish friend. He came home from his first evening at the club too excited to sleep. He read the magazines that had been pressed upon him there far into the night and, near dawn, wrote a free-verse poem to exorcise his tumultuous reactions.

When he was elected executive secretary of the club, in 1923, he joined the Communist party. He says he tried to be a good Communist. He had not been drawn to the Party by "the economics of Communism, nor the great power of trade unions, nor the excitement of underground politics. . . . [His] attention was caught by the similarity of the experience of workers in other lands, by the possibility of uniting scattered but kindred peoples into a whole." [6]

But the Party did not class him as a worker. It labeled him an intellectual, and he discovered that the Party was suspicious

6. Richard Wright, "Richard Wright," in Richard Crossman (ed.), *The God That Failed* (New York, 1952), 106.

of all intellectuals—that it was, indeed, suspicious of Richard Wright. In his own Party unit, a segregated cell located in the Black Belt of the South Side, even his black comrades seemed to consider him, as an intellectual, a curio.

The Party interfered with his writing, and he had joined it as a writer; he had, in fact, published in some Party magazines some of his poetry and in the *New Masses* an article about Joe Louis. He held that a writer should write. The Party held that a writer at best should combine writing with political activity; but, failing that, he should never shirk his assignments at the barricades. How very much in dead earnest the Party was in its proscription of art for politics Wright came to know by direct experience. He had started on his novel, his major undertaking, when the Party communicated to him its decision that he was to organize a committee on the high cost of living. He expostulated, citing his novel. The Party was adamant, and the novel suffered while he organized.

Nor was the Party, for all of its uniting of peoples, free of color prejudice. In 1935 Wright was sent as a delegate to a writers' congress in New York. The white delegates were lodged without incident through a local committee on arrangements. Wright had to shift for himself to find a place to sleep. One night he spent in the kitchen of a white couple who seemed to be friends of one of his white fellow Chicago Communists. He ended, the next night, in Harlem at the YMCA branch there.

Indeed, when all was taken into account Wright could not fail to notice a certain Gilbert-and-Sullivan derangement of the reasonable in much that the Party said and did. Only, the derangement was not intentional. It was not the consequence of levity or carelessness or, even, a spirit of high jinks. It was the result of solemn effort by solemn people, unconsciously acting as addled as lunatics. Actually, a man who claimed to be a painter did, on one occasion, appear from out of the void to join the Chicago John Reed Club while Wright was serving as its executive secretary, suggest that he had powerful connections within the Party, cause a great furor with extravagant and palpably unjustified charges against one of the club's most respected members, and, then, disappear with the club still somewhat intimidated by him before this tribune of the people was discovered to be nothing more or less than a lunatic from Detroit somehow free of his usual confinement. How could this happen? It was because of the way "normal" operations were actually conducted in the Party. And the Party could suit its words to its deeds. It could talk as fantastically as it behaved. It could, and did, prate of "counter-revolutionary activity," "incipient Trotskyites," "bastard intellectuals," "anti-leadership attitudes," and something called "seraphim tendencies," a phrase, Wright came to discover, which signified, within the Party, "that one has withdrawn from the struggle of life and finds himself infallible."

It was, Wright could hardly avoid observing, the good Communists who thought themselves infallible. If the Party had tagged Albert Einstein a "bastard intellectual," to a good Communist so Einstein would have been, despite the undeniable originality of some of his best-known feats of intellect. And all these things were of a piece with a Communist practice that, perhaps, nettled Wright most—the imputation by a Party leader to a lesser light of damaging remarks that the lesser light (and less powerful comrade) had actually never uttered.

In one reflective moment Wright concluded of the Party that much of its both startling and maddening tendency to act unrealistically before obvious realities was attributable to its history in Russia. Under the czars the Russian Communists were conspirators. They had to be suspicious of everything, for the police were unremittingly in hot pursuit of them. And conventionally conditioned American Communists were behaving in the America of the 1920s as did their ideological forebears in czarist Russia.

The Communists, Wright felt, had given him some good things. He felt that he had found among them his first sustained human relationships. His early years, then, with no father since before he started to school, a mother too soon invalided, only relatives of lesser consanguinity with whom he invariably bickered, and a largely malicious environment outside this none-too-congenial family circle, may well have been even lonelier than he was ever to care to admit. Certainly he felt that he had learned from the Communists. They had made, he believed, the first organized search for the truth about the oppressed, and he never seems to have lost his respect for the Communist knowledge-in-detail of the lives of the workers of the world; nor did he cease to appreciate the magnitude of the capacity with which communism would make "men feel the earth and the people on it."

For Communist social science, then, apparently, he retained always an intellectual's regard. So, too, he apparently remained always grateful to the Party for its tonic effect on some of his early writing. Given, he believed, a new knowledge of the great world by Communist materials and a new elevation of spirit by Communist ideals, he produced some of the first work that seemed to him to express what he wanted to say. But, in the final analysis, too much of Communist practice outraged both his sense of independence and his sense of sanity. He had declared himself inactive in the Party well before May Day of 1936, not without some unpleasant reactions from the Party, which he avers he tried to avoid. Apparently, his formal severance from Party membership did not come until 1944.

But by 1944 Wright was no longer living in Chicago. We may have seen that some poetry of his had been published. So, too, in 1936, had a novella of his in *New Caravan*. And we have seen, too, that he was planning, and trying to work on, a novel. This novel had become for him the thing that *must* be done. And so in May of 1937 he went east. He did not go without the knowledge that he was taking a risk which was all of his own making. He had taken a third civil service examination on which he had achieved virtually a perfect score. Just now, when he was nerving himself for the great *Putsch* at writing, notice reached him of his appointment to a permanent clerkship in the Chicago Post Office at $2,100 annually, a magnificent salary in 1937. Like Cortez at Vera Cruz, however, he chose to burn his bridges behind him and he hitchhiked for the second time to New York City.

In New York he worked again with the Federal Writers' Project. But he also worked at his writing and at trying to peddle his stories. He was not to be successful at selling his individual stories, but his novella "Big Boy Leaves Home," in 1937 won a prize in *Story* for the best story of the year, and Harper's printed four of his stories in *Uncle Tom's Children.* The book was a success. In 1939 Wright received a Guggenheim award to free him for creative work. In October, 1939, *Native Son* was published, and chosen as a dual selection of the Book-of-the-Month Club. The novel sold well instantly and brought him recognition as well as profit. The Spingarn Medal, annual award of the NAACP to an American Negro for preeminent achievement, was presented to him in 1940. In 1941 *Native Son* was made into a play, Wright collaborating with Paul Green in the transformation, and produced on Broadway under the direction of Orson Welles. The late Canada Lee took the lead role of Bigger Thomas, and the play had a run of fourteen weeks in the metropolis before it was taken on the road. There could be no doubt, Wright's lean years were over.

The lean years of his personal life were over too. In 1940 Wright had married Ellen Poplar, a Jewish girl of New York City. Their first child was a daughter, Julia, born in 1942, the same year in which Wright's third book, *12 Million Black Voices,* was published. He and his wife were living by then in Brooklyn, although Wright (accompanied by his first wife) had spent some time in 1940 in Mexico, working on a second novel related to life in New York City which he never finished.[7] He did finish, however, his own account of his early years, *Black Boy,* which was published in 1945. But World War II was ending now. Wright had hoped the peace would bring

7. This seems to have been the book which he also sometimes described as a novel about the status of woman.

greater changes in the treatment of minorities in America than he was able to discern. An invitation to reside in France was extended to him by the government of France. With his wife and Julia, after spending much of 1946 in the French capital, he forsook Greenwich Village, to which the Wrights had moved from Brooklyn, and went to Paris. It was 1947 and the second stage of his life, his stage of residence in the North, had run its course.

He never returned, except for one visit, to the United States. Gertrude Stein had found for him, in the Latin Quarter, a large apartment. He settled down in a city where he was free to go and come as he had never been in the United States. This Paris became his home, though France never became the land of his citizenship. He was an expatriate American, never a naturalized Frenchman. Nor was he ever a sedentary boulevardier. Before he left America, he had spent some time in Mexico, but also, in 1945, in Quebec. In 1950, he lived on his third continent, South America, where he went to the Argentine for the making, from the novel, *Native Son*, of a movie in which he played, without proving himself an actor, but also, only after having been drafted to do it, the role of Bigger Thomas. In Ghana, in 1953, he lived for some weeks on his fourth continent, Africa. His coverage of the Bandung Conference in 1955 carried him to Asia. He had set foot, then, on all the major land masses of the world except Australia. And he did move around, also in western Europe. He lectured, and visited, at various times, in Italy, Holland, Germany, Denmark, and the Scandinavian peninsula; and he made two extended trips to Spain for the writing of his *Pagan Spain*.

Yet he made only one serious attempt really to detach himself from his acquired Parisian background. In 1958 Julia was looking forward to going to college. A brilliant student with a most impressive scholastic record, the best in the lycee for her year, she received bids from Oxford and Cambridge. She chose Cambridge, but it was not deemed advisable for her to go there alone. Wright and his wife had had a second child in

1947, another daughter, born in France and speaking only French, whom they named Rachel. Ellen Wright and Rachel left Wright alone in France to accompany Julia to England. Wright had now to himself both the apartment in the Latin Quarter and a farm house near the village of Ailly on the river Eure in Normandy which he had bought in 1957 as a place to which he could retire from his exposed position in sociable Paris and have the solitude and leisure a working writer tends to need. It took him, who had long been a grown man before he acquired a felicitous domesticity, little time to make the decision to sell both the apartment and the house and cross the Channel to London. He received, of course, from the English the customary tourist's visa. But when he applied for the residence visa that would have permitted him to live in England with his wife and Rachel and thus join them in their nearness to Julia, he was surprised with a rejection. Friends of his in England interceded with the Home Office. He went himself there in person. The residence visa was not forthcoming. Convinced that the British did not truly want Negroes in Britain, though they also wanted not to seem not to want them, Wright returned to France, taking now an apartment in the rue Regis smaller than the one he had surrendered in anticipation of his move to England.

He had worked hard and published much during his years abroad: three novels, *Savage Holiday,* a "white" novel not about the race problem, *The Outsider,* and *The Long Dream;* and four books that were not fiction, *Black Power, Pagan Spain, The Color Curtain,* and *White Man, Listen!* Wright had also prepared for publication a collection of short stories, *Eight Men,* which would appear very shortly after his death. He had lectured before audiences in Europe, seen and unseen. He was beginning to write radio drama for German radio. He had learned about the special Japanese poetic form, haiku and was experimenting with the application of this Oriental aesthetic discipline to Negro material. He had even accepted an invitation from

Nicole Barclay to write for her Barclay's Disques, a French record company, the comment to accompany some of the recordings of jazz to be issued under that firm's name. Even without his family his days were full, for he was no recluse. He did more than write. He had helped in the organization of the Societe Africaine de Culture. He was interested in its magazine, *Presence Africaine.* He had friends and visitors, many of both undoubtedly eminent. Some were French like Sartre. Some were Americans living in Paris, like his good companion Ollie Harrington, whose cartoon character, Bootsie, may be the finest satire of its kind yet conceived by a Negro. Some were visiting foreigners, if any person of an intellectual or aesthetic bent can be called a foreigner in Paris. Some were very much like himself, Negro writers, but Negro writers who were remaining in America. Indeed, on an autumn day in 1960 Langston Hughes arrived to visit him and found him in his apartment fully clothed, but lying on a bed under cover. The spectacle before Hughes seemed to require a witticism, and Hughes laid under contribution an echo from the familiar vocabulary of the Negro evangelical faiths. "Man," he said, "You look like you're going to glory." Wright explained. There was no cause for alarm. In Africa, some years previously, he had contracted intestinal amoeba. Occasionally, therefore, it became wise for him to submit himself to a rather routine physical examination. He was merely waiting to be taken to the Eugene Gibez Clinic, had dressed for his journey, and had decided to rest while waiting for his transportation. Hughes seems to have been Wright's last visitor. On Monday night, November 28, 1960, Wright was still in the clinic, but awaiting his scheduled release to return to his apartment in the morning. His nurse had left him and he was alone when his night bell sounded. When the nurse responded, she found him dead. Death had claimed him suddenly and from a rather unexpected quarter. He had had a heart attack, not a fatal onslaught of the complaint which accounted for his presence in the hospital. He must have died almost instantaneously, conceivably even before the full portent of this final seizure from which there could be no appeal was apparent to him.

His body was cremated and his ashes quietly interred in a locker at the famed cemetery Pere la Chaise. It is a far cry from a Negro hovel in the Mississippi Delta to the inner haunts of an international aristocracy of talent in Paris, that *bon vivant's* elysium of the Western artist-intellectual. Indeed, it is a cry so very "far," in a certain sense of psychic distance, as thus alone to constitute a fairly reliable index of the dauntlessness of Richard Wright's resolution and of the indefatigability of his enterprise—as well as, it may be added, of the extraordinary range of his overt experience of life. For the Richard Wright whom Hamlet's fell sergeant arrested so prematurely at such a great remove from his ancestral roots had achieved a miracle of sorts. He had conquered as his own Odysseus much more than land and sea, in the literal sense. He had really conquered, in effect, a succession of social worlds, and the truly significant pilgrimage he had managed to negotiate had been his migration in progressive stages of advance from the despised universe of the American folk Negro across formidable barriers of custom and privilege into virtually a white man's status in a particularly privileged enclave of the white man's world.

Hence, undoubtedly we should give a most attentive ear to Wright when, in *Black Boy*, apropos the confrontation that became eventually his final meeting with his father (as it was, at its occurrence on a Mississippi plantation, his first in almost precisely a quarter of a century), after speaking of his father "standing alone upon the red clay . . . a sharecropper, clad in ragged overalls, holding a muddy hoe in his gnarled, veined hands,"[8] he proceeds to declare:

[When] I tried to talk to him [my own father] I realized that, though ties of blood made us kin, though I could see a shadow of my face in

8. Richard Wright, *Black Boy* (New York, 1945), 30.

his face, though there was an echo of my voice in his voice, *we were forever strangers, speaking a different language, living on vastly distant planes of reality* [italics mine].[9]

We should, that is, note carefully Wright's own insistence, in terms that brook no equivocation, upon the great and irreconcilable cultural abyss between himself and his unreconstructed parent. We should acknowledge, too, the ample apparent warrant for the lack of compromise in Wright's depiction of his position relative to his father. After all, Wright had written one book about Spain, another about a country in Africa, a third which dealt with the Bandung Conference, of which he had been an eye witness. Some of his short stories have European settings. One of his novels, even though it is his poorest, departs altogether from racism and its pitifully circumscribed areas of preoccupation. He clearly could not have written what he did write had he lived a life too much like that of his father. Nor could he, for that matter, have married as he married, or talked as he came to talk, or thought as he came to think. An immensity of cultural variation did sunder him from his father, a whole buoyant mass of learned responses in concepts and behavior, for the assimilation of which he had, in all their blooming welter, discovered a more or less varying capacity, but of the nature and uses of which his father had not the slightest inkling.

And yet ours is, when everything is said and done, a curious and inconsistent world in which, as an aspect of its sometimes inscrutably organic complexity, it is possible for two propositions, which seem to cancel each other out in their abstract logic, both to be empirically true and each to make the other, empirically, even truer. Just so, as there does seem to be, incontrovertibly, good reason to aver of Wright and his father that they ended by becoming, toward each other, in all obvious respects, like total strangers, and evidence just as compelling for the contention that their alienation from each other was

9. *Ibid.*

the almost unavoidably inescapable consequence of differences in the worlds into which they were cast as their lives continued, so it seems equally valid to maintain that they were linked together by a bond that could never be severed and to argue that, in spite of the noticeable impact upon Wright of conditioning factors from the white worlds into which he had been able to insinuate himself, this bond was forged out of Wright's fellowship with his father in the world of the American Negro masses.

That fellowship dated, of course, from the moment Wright drew his first breath. It extended on Wright's side, however, actively only through the years of his youth, the formative years for any individual born into the human family, the plastic years during which all creatures so originated tend to acquire the deep-seated basic reactions that shape their characters for the remainder of their lives. Such years obviously are of no little import in the personal history of every person ever socialized. In the development of creative writers, whose trade depends to a considerable extent upon exceptional receptivity to stimuli from an external world, these very years are probably even more than ordinarily meaningful. Certainly, James Baldwin, who knew Wright on two continents and for more than half of Wright's adult life, found a special significance in those years where Wright was concerned. For Baldwin once observed of Wright—in comparing, incidentally, Wright's sense of reality with the fondness of Sartre and Sartre's circle for ideal speculation—"I always sensed in Richard Wright a Mississippi pickaninny, mischievous, cunning and tough. This seemed to be at the bottom of everything he did, like some fantastic jewel buried in high grass." [10] And while it is true that Baldwin here is making no issue of race, but merely playing upon a racial epithet to heighten the impression he wishes to convey of a Wright educated early, and lastingly, in a particularly bitter school of hard knocks, it is also true that Baldwin's contention

10. James Baldwin, *Nobody Knows My Name* (New York, 1961), 184.

opposes any conception of Wright as a creature totally emancipated from the world to which Wright's father still belonged
when the father and son faced each other as we have been told
they did in *Black Boy*. If we are to credit Baldwin, then even at
this last meeting Wright and his father were not total strangers.
They did not live on vastly different planes of reality. It may
have seemed that they did, and in much that was most percepti-
ble, even to Wright himself, no other conclusion may have appeared reasonable. Yet Baldwin's phrase may haunt us, may
tease us into further thought.

Mississippi pickaninny! It is an apt phrase. And it is even
apter if we read it with a keen awareness both of its implications
of Wright's indestructible affinities with his own youth and of
his membership, which was irrevocable, in a peculiarly racial
world. We may wish then, perhaps, to ponder deeply Redding's
words, written soon after Wright's death: "In going to live
abroad, Dick Wright had cut the roots that once sustained him;
the tight-wound emotional core had come unravelled; the
creative center had dissolved," [11] and to add thereto Redding's
veritable extension of those remarks a year later — "His heart's
home [Wright's] and his mind's tether was in America. It is
not the America of the moving pictures, nor of Thomas Wolfe,
John P. Marquand and John O'Hara's novels, nor of the
histories of the Allan Nevins and C. J. H. Hayes. It is the
America that only Negroes know: a ghetto of the soul, a bound-
ary of the mind, a confine of the heart." [12] For it may well be
that Baldwin and Redding, in their separate fashions, have
both pointed the way to the indispensable prelude for an
understanding of Richard Wright, conceivably as a person,
and certainly as a literary artist. It may well be that the picture
of Wright which one should bear most in mind is not that of a
Wright so visibly grown away from his father as to seem a

11. J. Saunders Redding, "Richard Wright: An Evaluation," *Amsac Newsletter*,
III (December, 1940), 6.
12. J. Saunders Redding, "Home Is Where the Heart Is," *New Leader* (December 11, 1961), 24.

visitor from another world as the father and the son finally encounter each other for a strained brief moment under a southern sun, but rather the child described by Baldwin, and confirmed as a presence by Redding, who lurked always at the center of Wright's mind and heart, the child whose only real abode was the "America that only Negroes know," and whose only real release came in the fictive world of Wright's creation closest to the actual world that Wright had known in the Negro subculture of his youth.

Richard Wright
in a Moment
of Truth

AS I *remember it, I tinkered for some months with the ideas and content that are given shape in "Richard Wright in a Moment of Truth" and read it in slightly variant forms at several places before its appearance in the* Southern Literary Journal *in the spring of 1971.*

I was very glad to have it accepted by the Southern Literary Journal. *There seems to me great merit in reminding people that Wright was a southern writer. A great deal has been said about Faulkner's Mississippi. No sensitive person, I think, would have it otherwise. The quality of Faulkner's art guarantees that. But no informed sensitive person, I also like to think, would care to ignore Wright's Mississippi or to forget that Wright's Mississippi asserts itself not only in the fiction Wright located in Mississippi settings but also in whatever he wrote wherever he went. Mississippi was his home as much as it was Faulkner's, and southern literature must claim them both and put energy and wisdom into understanding them both.*

ᗢᗦ

Many people, if not most, perhaps never associate Richard Wright with the state of Mississippi, which is another way of saying that they do not associate him with the South. He was, however, a Mississippian, a southerner, and to call him that is not merely to demand due recognition for the statistics of his birth and residence during his plastic years, but also to recognize a fact of the utmost importance in understanding the growth and peculiarities of his artistic imagination. Richard

Wright remains best known as the author of *Native Son*. Four years before *Native Son*, however, he had published a novella, which he called "Big Boy Leaves Home." It is on this earlier and relatively unnoticed novella that I wish to evangelize.

"Big Boy Leaves Home" is a story that proceeds from beginning to end as a simple, straight-line narrative. Mechanically, at least, it is assembled like a play, detachable into five episodes, each as clearly discrete as a scene in a formal drama, and each, along the time-scheme of the novella, placed somewhat later than its immediate predecessor, until the action, at the point which in a theater would ring down the final curtain, conveys Big Boy, the story's protagonist, northward toward Chicago, hidden in the covered back of a truck.

The first episode breathes something of the atmosphere of a rural Eden. On a clear, warm day in Mississippi four self-indulgent Negro boys are discovered in a wood on the outskirts of the little town in which they and their families reside. The boys are Big Boy and his constant companions Lester, Buck, and Bobo. It becomes quickly obvious that Big Boy is the natural leader of the four and the constant recipient of hero-worship from the other three. It becomes equally obvious that the four should not be where they are, for it is a school day and they are decidedly of school age. They are, then, young rebels giving full vent to some of their rebellious tendencies. And yet it does not appear that they are criminally inclined. They are, rather, healthy and high-spirited cousins-german of Huck Finn, with a proper ambivalence of attitude toward the queer world of adults and a proper interest in enjoying their youth while they still have it to enjoy. They are not, it must be confessed, altogether nice by the standards of a Little Lord Fauntleroy. Their language, for example, runs to words not used in polite child-rearing circles. Their sense of fun expresses itself too often in the sadistic exploitation of some defenseless victim's physical discomfiture. They know, too, about sex, and not through programs of sex education. Even so, they cannot be classed as juvenile delinquents. Nothing about them stamps

them as young practitioners of vice and violence. But just as un-
deniably they cannot be classed as adults. To recognize this is
of the utmost importance in a reading of their story. They like
to try to act like grown-ups. What normal adolescents do not?
Nevertheless, as adults, they are actually only innocents,
actually only ingénus uninitiated into most of what are often
called "the facts of life." To be classed as adults, they have
still seen far too little of the scattered and extensive middens
of corruption that tend to separate in a most decisive manner
prototypical adulthood from even the latest phase of nonadult-
hood. Their innocence does not make them as pure as the
driven snow. But it does permit them still to think and act like
irresponsible children. And it is as irresponsible children, out
for a children's lark, that they suddenly, and capriciously,
decide to quit their wood (one is strongly tempted to say their
enchanted forest) and go swimming—trespassing on the land
and in the pond of Ol Man Harvey, a white man noted for his
lack of love for Negroes and, not incidentally, noted especially
to them for his aversion to their swimming in his pond.

The second episode takes them, consequently, from their
open wood to Ol Man Harvey's pond. For a golden moment it is
as if they had not left the wood, as if they are still, as it were,
in the innocent world of their enchanted youth. They swim, ap-
propriately for innocents, in the nude. They have, at least
temporarily, abandoned swimming and are sunning themselves, still nude, on the beach of Ol Man Harvey's pond when
they look up and find a white woman whom they do not know
and who does not know them, fixedly regarding them from a
spot on the pond's opposite bank. Abruptly their story has
changed worlds. It has crossed a line. Clearly the woman
watching them is already virtually on the verge of hysteria.
They try to prevent an apparently all-too-impending disaster,
to assure the strange white woman, who looms between them
and their clothes, that all they want is to get those clothes and
depart the pond in peace. But this woman is not part of the
world of the beginning of their story. She belongs to the world

controlled and interpreted by adults. In that world, at least
when "Big Boy Leaves Home" was written, all Negro males,
even young and with their clothes on, were potential rapists.
And so this woman screams, and screams again, for someone
named Jim, and Jim himself, a white man from her world,
comes apace, with a rifle in his hands. He asks no questions and
pauses not at all to profit from a single bit of rational analysis.
Instead, he fires and kills two of the potential rapists, Buck
and Lester, instantly. But Bobo and Big Boy, in a manner of
speaking, have better luck. They survive the white man's initial
barrage. Swiftly a moment of violent confusion ensues, and
then ends, with the white man's rifle somehow in Big Boy's
hands. Unable, as he sees it, under the circumstances to resort
to any other method of deterrence, Big Boy fatally shoots the
white man and he and Bobo, with their clothes and the now-
expendable garments of Buck and Lester, vanish in the direction of the town.

The third episode changes the setting from a white adult
world to a black. Big Boy has managed to make his way home to
his own house. Presumably, so has Bobo. At Big Boy's house his
parents and his sister now are told about the terrible thing
which has happened at the pond. Hastily they summon, for
advice and counsel, a handful of the respected elders of their
local black community. The elders summoned decide that Big
Boy perforce must hide himself for the night in one of a set of
pits dug for kilns on the side of a hill overlooking a main high-
way known as Bullard's Road. Word is to be sent to Bobo to
join Big Boy in hiding there. At six in the morning Will
Sanders, a son of one of the counseling elders, will pick the two
boys up. By a fortuitous coincidence Will is already scheduled,
just after the approaching dawn, to drive a load of goods to
Chicago for his employer, a trucking company.

In the fourth episode Big Boy does reach the prescribed
hill safely and does conceal himself deep within a chosen pit.
He is waiting now for Bobo. Darkness comes, but no Bobo.
What does, however, arrive at last, direfully impinging itself

upon Big Boy's consciousness, is a mob that gathers on a hill directly across the road from the one in which he is concealed and from which he can hardly fail to see, as from a seat within the mezzanine of a theater or concert hall, virtually any atrocity that the mob may intend to perpetrate. And the mob does perpetrate a major atrocity. It has captured Bobo and it brings him to its hill. As Big Boy watches, helpless to intervene or withdraw, it proceeds there, on its hill, to tar and feather Bobo, and to burn him at the stake. Then, as a rain begins to fall, the mob, its baser appetites assuaged, melts away in small groups into the night.

The fifth, and final, episode is muted and brief. Morning comes, and with it, unobtrusively parked on Bullard's Road, Will Sanders' truck, into which, collected from his night-long perch, Big Boy is safely stowed and thus spirited away to Chicago, famished and thirsty, and bereft forever of the kind of innocence which had still been largely his before the incident at Old Man Harvey's pond.

"Big Boy Leaves Home" was accepted for publication in the spring of 1936. It seems to have been actually written down in the summer and fall of 1935. It seems also to have a discernible prehistory to which I wish now to allude, for reasons that I trust will appear as I proceed.

Richard Wright fled the South in 1927, two months after his nineteenth birthday. He came directly to Chicago, where, by 1932, led by his enthusiastic attachment to a John Reed Club, he had become a Communist. His Communist affiliation brought him eventually into association with a fellow Communist who, like himself, was a Negro born and bred at a considerable distance below the Mason-Dixon Line. Wright speaks of the black fellow Communist, under the almost certain alias of Ben Ross, in Wright's version of his own experience of communism, which he originally contributed, under the title "I Tried To Be a Communist," to the *Atlantic Monthly* in 1944.

This so-called Ross, who had a Jewish wife, the mother, by him, of a young son, interested Wright deeply. Wright saw

Ross as "a man struggling blindly between two societies," and felt that if he "could get . . . Ross' story . . . he could make known some of the difficulties in the adjustment of a folk people to an urban environment." [1] Therefore, he persuaded Ross, in effect, to sit for a pen portrait. On occasion he interviewed Ross for hours in Ross's home. Meanwhile, however, the Communist command in Chicago had become cognizant of Wright's interest in Ross and had begun to view this interest with mounting concern. Once aware of the Party's apprehensions, Ross ceased to speak freely to Wright either of his life or of himself. This inhibition of Ross's responsiveness sabotaged Wright's original hopes. Wright had met some of Ross's friends and, expanding on his original plan, had conceived the notion now of doing, with Ross and Ross's friends all in mind, a series of biographical sketches. Now, however, not only Ross but all of Ross's friends as well had become afraid to talk to Wright as Wright had once had ample reason to suppose they might. Wright consequently altered his intentions.

In virtually Wright's own words, after he saw that he could do nothing to counteract the effect of the Party's powerful influence, he merely sat and listened to Ross and his friends tell tales of southern Negro experience, noting them down in his mind, no longer daring to ask questions for fear his informants would become alarmed. In spite of his informants' reticence, Wright became drenched in the details of their lives. He gave up the idea of writing biographical sketches and settled finally upon writing a series of short stories, using the material he had got from Ross and his friends, building upon it and inventing from it. Thus he wove a tale of a group of black boys trespassing upon the property of a white man and the lynching that followed. The story was published eventually under the title of "Big Boy Leaves Home." [2]

Corroboration of Wright's direct testimony in "I Tried To Be a Communist," and some further suggestions concerning

1. Wright, "Richard Wright," Crossman (ed.), *The God That Failed*, 115.
2. *Ibid.*, 119–20.

the genesis of "Big Boy Leaves Home," are supplied in Constance Webb's recent biography of Wright.[3] This biography, it is of some significance here to note, bears the character of an official life. Indeed, in the book's introduction Miss Webb so defines the nature of what she has done in no uncertain terms. In this introduction, that is to say, she first makes specific allusion to her personal friendship with Wright and his family, a friendship which began, she tells us, when Wright was at work on *Black Boy* in the early 1940s and lasted until his death. She cites the many materials — notes, letters, telegrams, manuscripts, ideas for new books — which, from the time of her decision in 1945 to compose a study of him and his work and in full knowledge of her plans, Wright delivered to her over a period of fifteen years. She also refers to her many long hours of conversation with Wright in New York City, on Long Island, and in Paris; to her continuing relations with Wright's wife after his untimely death; to the assistance provided her by Wright's brother Alan, Wright's close boyhood friend Joe C. Brown, and Wright's literary agent, Paul R. Reynolds, Jr.; to the aid given her by an impressive number of Wright's fellow authors and other acquaintances who were in a position to speak of Wright with some authority; and, finally in this present context, to the access granted her by Wright and his family to hundreds of letters from Wright to his editor, Edward C. Aswell.

With these credentials, which are not to be summarily dismissed, Miss Webb positively identifies the pseudonymous Ben Ross as one David Poindexter, a black member of the Communist party, who had been born in southwest Tennessee in 1903 and had come north when he was seventeen. The family attributed by Miss Webb to Poindexter is the same as that attributed by Wright to Ross. In all the other details that she stipulates, moreover, including Poindexter's status as the original of Big Boy, Miss Webb assimilates Poindexter to the person whom Wright, conceivably in order not to expose a friend

3. Constance Webb, *Richard Wright* (New York, 1968).

and benefactor to possible jeopardy, named as Ross in "I Tried To Be a Communist." But when she reports directly on the genesis of "Big Boy Leaves Home," [4] Miss Webb does not parrot what Wright had once said about his determination, if he could, to use Poindexter, or Ross, as an instrument by means of which he could make known some of the difficulties attendant upon the adjustment of a folk people to an urban environment. In this context, as a matter of fact, she makes a statement that would seem to contradict Wright's own about the folk. She says, instead and unequivocally, that in his first series of short stories, *Uncle Tom's Children* (the series of which "Big Boy Leaves Home" became a part), Wright set himself a conscious problem: the explication of the quality of will the Negro must possess to live and die in a country which denies him his humanity.[5] Furthermore, applying her statement to "Big Boy Leaves Home" specifically, she asserts, within her analysis of that story, that "Big Boy Leaves Home" represents this quality of will as being "only that of the most elemental level—the ability to endure," [6] for, she finally adds, the lesson to be extracted from Big Boy's experience is the dependence of his survival "upon the communal nature of the black community which planned, aided, and organized an escape." [7]

When she says that Wright, in creating "Big Boy Leaves Home" and the other stories in *Uncle Tom's Children*, "set himself a conscious problem," the significant word is *conscious*. She has left no doubt, as I have already indicated, of her conception of her relationship with Wright. He made of her, according to her implication, an alter ego privy to virtually all of himself that he could communicate to anyone. Furthermore, although the word *conscious* does not appear in her declaration that Big Boy's story was planned to demonstrate how his community rallied round him to ensure the preservation of his life, it

4. *Ibid.*, 125.
5. *Ibid.*, 157.
6. *Ibid.*, 159.
7. *Ibid.*

seems unmistakably clear that here she speaks, too, as a medium who is reporting not only what was in Wright's mind, but also what, she would contend, he *knew* was there. Here, then, is testimony, much of it of a hearsay nature indeed, but nevertheless purporting, in its general trend, to have the value of evidence which Wright himself could not have failed to give had he ever had to speak about the intended function of "Big Boy" under solemn oath in a court of law. It reveals, to repeat for emphasis, that Wright had chosen a definite thing to do when he wrote "Big Boy Leaves Home," and that he was not confused as to the nature of that thing. It seems to argue also Wright's own belief that he had substantially achieved his conscious intent.

Writers, however, sometimes belie their own intentions. Sometimes, moreover, what they do actually may well seem better than what they thought they had intended. No one, I think, would argue seriously for a reading of "Big Boy Leaves Home" as an account of an adjustment by an agrarian folk to an urban setting, deeply interested though Wright once indicated that he was in Ross/Poindexter and drenched though he once was in Ross/Poindexter's life and history. If then, however, "Big Boy Leaves Home" is to be read primarily as a parable about the quality of will necessary for the Negro to solve the major problem he faces in his American environment, and if the message of such a parable centers in an account of the manner in which one Negro community expressed the quality of its will through its capacity to save some of its own, then neither the form nor the content of the parable is aesthetically impressive. "Big Boy Leaves Home" becomes then only an exercise in the depiction of a failure. Its focal point, if not its climax, must then be found to be in its third episode, for in this episode the representatives of the Negro community do gather, in Big Boy's home. The preacher, Elder Peters, is there, and Brother Jenkins and Brother Sanders, with Big Boy's parents and his sister. They commune with each other. But with what results? Big Boy's father can only berate Big Boy on the folly of his disobedience to his mother's injunction to go to school. The women in the house can only watch the men gather there in virtually unbroken silence. No one can respond affirmatively to the distressed father's plea for financial aid. The sister has done some service in bringing to the house the three outside counselors. The mother gives Big Boy simple food to take with him when he leaves. Still, it is chance alone and Big Boy's own animal excellences that pave the way for his escape from certain death. No effective aid reaches Bobo. No account is taken of provisions to safeguard Big Boy's family, who, as Big Boy later overhears in his kiln, are burned out of their modest dwelling. The most that can be said finally is that Big Boy did elude his would-be slayers and that a fellow Negro, who happened to be going in that direction anyhow, drove him north.

But whatever Wright's original conscious aims, to read "Big Boy Leaves Home" in accord with the form dictated for it by its own development, and to sense its content shaping itself to match that form and its function emerging as the strong, inevitable concomitant of both, is to witness what well may be one of the three or four finest moments in Negro fiction. On this inherent form and content it is now high time to comment.

It will be remembered that Big Boy's story is shaped into five episodes, five scenes conducting a flow of action and related meaning from a point of attack to a conclusion that should round out and justify the whole. This form is flexible as well as fluid. It permits variations of pitch and tone and atmosphere which all contribute to the story's total impact. At the beginning the pitch is moderate. The tone and atmosphere are genial, almost sweet. The function of the content is expository. The identity of the protagonist is established and the condition of all four of the boys made known. And beyond all this a theme is adumbrated. For these boys are scholars out of school. They have interrupted their vocation for a holiday of their own making. Still, the fact is clear. They are young, much untaught, and at an impressionable age. To learn, to grow, in other words, in one way or another, is their *metier*. It is hard to see how they should live through any single day without acquiring some new knowledge. In what they are reside the germs of what this tale must be. Then comes the first progression, bringing with itself a proper set of changes. At the swimming hole the white world intrudes. The mood of the first episode is shattered by the killings. In a swirl of strident sound and emotions at high pitch and harshly tuned, with corresponding action that is equally cacophonous, a motif of pain and mystery, the ugliness of racist custom, is introduced. Then comes an interlude with a reduction in pitch and a moderation of tone, but without a return to the relative serenity of the introduction, as Big Boy spends a moment with his own kind in his father's house. But this interlude is also prelude, and a fitting one, to the big scene of the story. This big scene, as the logic of the story would demand, is the lynching on the hill, the spectacle of Bobo coated with hot tar and white feathers, burning in the night. This, as we shall see in terms of content, is the moment of truth in the story. It is also the very peak of the wave of form, when pitch and tone and atmosphere all coalesce at their highest points. The story cannot end at such a level of crescendo and fortissimo. It does not; it declines to the low key of its final episode when Big Boy, all passion spent, drifts off to slumber on the bed of the truck that bears him away to the North.

But let us return to the lynching on the hill. I have said that for this story it is the moment of truth. And it is. It is the moment when Wright, whether wittingly or not, gathers up the essence of that which he is struggling to express and stores it all into one symbol and its attendant setting. For the spectacle of Bobo aflame at the stake does constitute a symbol. It is a symbol, moreover, the phallic connotations of which cannot be denied. Indeed, the particularity of its detail—the shape of its mass, its coating of tar, the whiteness of the feathers attached to its surface or floating out into the surrounding air—are almost all too grossly and gruesomely verisimilar for genteel contemplation. Whether Wright so intended it or not, the lynching of Bobo is symbolically a rite of castration. It is the ultimate indignity that can be inflicted upon an individual. Such an indignity strips from a man his manhood, removes from him the last vestige of his power and the last resort of his self-respect. In the lynching of Bobo, thus, all lynchings are explained, and all race prejudice. Both are truly acts of castration. It is not for nothing that the grinning darky, hat in hand and bowing low, his backside exposed as if for a kick in the buttocks, seems so much a eunuch. He has accepted in his heart the final abasement, the complete surrender of his will, and so of his citadel of self, to anyone with a white skin. He has capitulated to the most arrogant demand one human creature can make upon another.

This, then, is the true anatomy of racism. It makes no difference where or how it proffers its claims, whether in an apology for its own being so adroitly composed as the novel *So Red the Rose* or in the blatant conduct of the old-style, sheeted Ku Klux Klan. What racism demands is that every white man should be permitted to reserve the right to visit, with impunity, upon any Negro whatever, any outrage of that Negro's personality the white man chooses to impose. This, then, is the symbolism of Bobo's burning body on the hill.

But around that symbolism clusters another set of facts put into another pregnant image. For, as Bobo burning illustrates the essence of one indispensable aspect of racism, the mob illustrates another. It is an efficient mob, a homogeneous grouping. Yet no one has really organized it. It has no officers and no carefully compiled manual of behavior. Still it operates like a watchmaker universe. Its members know what they are supposed to do, and they do it, as if they were performing the steps of a ritual dance—which of course they are. For that is the real secret of the people gathered around Bobo on his Golgotha. They are responding not only to xenophobia and to an obscene lust for power. They are responding also to an urge equally Neanderthal in its origins. They are acting tribally, even as every lodge brother, black or white or yellow or red, who ever gave a secret handshake and every Babbitt who ever applauded a toastmaster's feeble attempts at jollity at the luncheon of his service club.

To belong, to conform, and thus to avoid the existentialist nightmare of exercising the prerogative of individual freedom of choice; to be able to contribute all of one's own release of foible and malice to custom that must be followed for the good of the community; to accept the myth that at some time in the misty past a voice, as it were, from some local Sinai spoke to the elders of the tribe and told them how certain things must be done and what prescribed rites must be followed to avert the anger of the gods; thus to be exempted from a sense of guilt at one's own evil; thus to hallow the meanest of the herd instincts; thus to institutionalize mediocrity's hatred of the indomitable spirit and its envy of strength and beauty: this is the pathos, and yet an important part of the explanation, of the tribe's capacity to survive. This is also as much a part of racism as is the lust for power. The castration and the tribalism complement each other. Without either, racism would not be at all what it is. To perceive them, to really take them in, is, as Henry James might say, to see and know what is *there*. And it is part of the excellence of form in this story that Big Boy does see them, that by the story's own arrangement he is positioned so that he cannot do otherwise. For, as this story so manages the sense of form that shapes its episodes to place its big scene right, it regulates concurrently another element of form, its control of its own point of view, to the end that at the proper point in the narrative's development the impression it conveys of who is doing the seeing will be as right as the prominence and the substance of what is to be seen.

Thus at the beginning of the story we are aware of, and share, to some extent, the consciousness of all the boys. But this is Big Boy's story. It is really his loss of innocence and compulsory education under special circumstances that this story embodies. And so, increasingly, as the story moves from the

open country to the lynching on the hill, Big Boy's consciousness becomes the sole point of view. Yet this constriction and
this concentration are really the ultimate outgrowth of a rather
delicate continuous maneuver of adjustment. We watch the
characters perform. We hear them talk. From outside their
consciousnesses we infer their thoughts and feelings. Yet we
identify increasingly with Big Boy, if for no other reason than
that we see nothing which he cannot see and hear nothing
which he cannot hear. But after Big Boy bids adieu to his
parents and their friends and, successfully negotiating his
sprint through hostile territory to Bullard's Road, comes to bay
at last crouched deep within his kiln, we become more and
more intensely one with him. We wonder with him why Bobo
has not come, share with him his memory of the events of his
day, mourn with him for Buck and Lester, regret with him that
he did not bring his father's shotgun, and finally, in fantasy,
imagine with him that he is blasting away with that shotgun as
he withstands a mob. As white men searching for the Negro
"bastards" drift down *his* hill we share, too, his fear; and finally,
as the lynch mob gathers, our senses become, like his, preter-
naturally acute, to watch with him in anguish the torture and
destruction of his last close boyhood friend. Thus the heightening and the concentration of the point of view join with the
elevation of the episode and the power of the symbolism and
the imagery to speak in blended voices acting in mighty concert
of the inner nature of racism and to trace its roots deep down
into the past of human psychology and custom.

It is not a quality of the Negro will that this story explicates,
nor is it anything to do with folk adjustment in a city. Far from
either. It is, rather, the psychology, and the anthropology, of
American racism. It is a lesson given to Big Boy and through
him to the world at large. It is a lesson, moreover, which
rounds off beautifully both the form and substance of "Big
Boy Leaves Home." For the plot of this story represents a
progress, not a conflict. Its succession of vignettes combine to
form a curious kind of sentimental journey in which Big Boy

does leave home — does lose, that is, his relative state of innocence — and does experience an illumination, an exercise in education, that provides him with a terrible, but highly freighted,
insight into the adult world.

It has been rather customary not to think of Richard Wright
as a southern writer, except, of course, by the accident of his
birth. I cannot share that view. A writer belongs, I would argue,
in the final analysis, to the country where his artistic imagination is most at home. Wright clearly supposed that this country,
for him, was not the South, just as he supposed that in "Big
Boy Leaves Home," in spite of the resemblances between Ol
Man Harvey's pond and the pond in Jackson, Mississippi,
around which Wright had played in his own youth, he was
writing about Ross/Poindexter and, in a philosophic vein,
either about a folk people seeking a new adjustment in a setting
alien to their past or struggling for self-gratifying survival
against a powerful outer world hostile to their hopes. Indeed,
in one of the major episodes of *Black Boy*, his own account of
his youth and early manhood, Wright tells of his last encounter
with his father, an encounter that occurred after twenty-five
years of absolute separation, as well as, also, after Wright had
published *Native Son*. He meets his father on a Mississippi
hillside. He tries to talk to him and then he says, "I realized
that, though ties of blood made us kin, though I could see a
shadow of my face in his face, though there was an echo of my
voice in his voice, we were forever strangers, speaking a different language, living on vastly different planes of reality." On
one level of interpretation Wright here does speak true. Between him and his father, time and experience had fixed an
impenetrable gulf. But the possibly implied symbolism of the
confrontation is false. Deep at the core of his own being,
whether as a person or as an artist, Wright always remained
his own Big Boy who never did leave home, and it was always
true that the closer he could get to the homeland of his youth,
which was also the homeland of his creative skill, the happier
he was in the fiction he was able to produce.

Wright's last considerable essay into fiction was his final novel, *The Long Dream*. In startling ways it reproduces all the significant elements of "Big Boy Leaves Home." Its setting is a Mississippi town and, incidentally, one which, for all of his obvious intentions to have it otherwise, he does not update from the Mississippi he quitted as a youth. Its protagonist is a Negro boy as exceptional among his peers as Big Boy is among his. Moreover, this boy too is in the process of growing up, for *The Long Dream*, like "Big Boy Leaves Home," is an initiation story. Fire figures prominently in the drama of *The Long Dream*. Indeed, fire repeatedly plays a mythopoeic role in Wright's important fiction, as in the furnace of *Native Son* or the collision of electrically driven monsters in the subway wreck of *The Outsider*. The Negro elders of "Big Boy Leaves Home" reappear in the protagonist's father, the doctor, the madam, the mistress, and the father's helper of *The Long Dream*. They are no more potent in the latter work than in the former. They have neither the grace nor the glory of the father in "Fire and Cloud" or the mother in "Bright and Morning Star." The strange white woman who precipitates catastrophe for the protagonist of "Big Boy Leaves Home" precipitates catastrophe also for the protagonist in *The Long Dream*. And, as at the end of "Big Boy Leaves Home," Big Boy is headed for another life in another world, so at the end of *The Long Dream* its protagonist is on a plane *en route* to Paris. The real difference, indeed, between "Big Boy Leaves Home" and *The Long Dream* is in the relative quality of the art of each.

Can we fail here to recall James Baldwin's reference to Wright as a "Mississippi pickaninny"? Baldwin was here comparing Wright with the Existentialists with whom Wright, in his later life, found himself consorting in Paris, and was thus paying genuine respect to a capacity in Wright to see life as it actually is and not according to some evanescent theory—a quality Baldwin thought he could divine in Wright, but not in Sartre and his disciples, and which Baldwin, in pensive mood, attributed to the lessons Wright had learned during his rough-

and-tumble existence as a boy and precocious adolescent in the Delta South. I think the phrase is apt. For Wright was a child of his own youth. Out of that youth he derived not only his practical sense of hard reality but also the home country for his artistic imagination. Thus, in much more than the mere statistics of his place of birth is he a southern writer. When he follows his home country north, as he does in the first two books of *Native Son,* he is still on his native ground. When he tries to return to it, as in *The Long Dream,* seeing it through eyes other than his own, he has deserted the one source of his greatest strength. He has become, that is, in all too sad a consequence, his own Big Boy away from home.

A Review of
J. L. Dillard's
Black English

I DID *this review, by request, for the* Journal of Negro History.

⊱⊰

The latest widely noticed discussion of American Negro speech is that which may be examined in J. L. Dillard's recently published extended statement, *Black English: Its History and Usage in the United States.* This book, to which I shall hereinafter refer as *Black English,* is what might well be called a scholar's report, and that is one thing; but it is also a prescription for social action, and that is something else altogether.

Dillard is white. I am black, a Negro. And so I think it only fair to say, *ab initio,* that I agree with Dillard in none of his major conclusions. I am unhappy also with his eulogizing of William A. Stewart, with whom he says that his exchange of information since 1965 has been so continuous that the book "might almost be viewed as a loose collaboration"[1] and to whom he gives the lion's share of credit for what Dillard insists is, or almost is, the first serious study of American Negro speech of any consequence. Nevertheless, I would like also to be able, without deluding myself, to believe that I reject Dillard's arguments not because he is white — as is Stewart — or because I find much associated with Stewart unsettling, or even because Dillard may seem to me an incompetent scholar, if not also a

---

1. J. L. Dillard, *Black English: Its History and Usage* (New York: Random House, 1972), xiii.

would-be self-aggrandizing opportunist. As a matter of fact, for everyone with any genuine interest in American Negro life, I believe that *Black English* constitutes an excursion into the ghetto and its environs well worth taking. However one reacts to the vistas it unfolds, or to Dillard's interpretations of those vistas, it is rooted in at least two realities. Enough Negroes say many, or most, of the things that Dillard says they say to justify a book like *Black English*. And Dillard himself is no tyro in his field. He is a thoroughly trained linguist who has immersed himself deeply and sensitively in the culture of the people he is studying. He must be credited also with an impressive general academic knowledge of the Negro. The bibliography at the end of *Black English* — a bibliography which a reading of *Black English* will demonstrate contains many items highly familiar to Dillard — could not have been assembled by someone whose acquaintance with his subject and its implications was superficial.

As a scholar's report *Black English* espouses a theory which Dillard stoutly maintains corresponds closely to factual veracity. At the heart of the theory is the proposition that there is in America a special and distinctive language that can be called Black English. Dillard, of course, contends that such a language does exist. He attributes to it unique qualities. He argues that the mere possession of these qualities makes Black English a separate language. He reminds us that the language from which Black English is most significantly separate is Standard English. And he says that four out of every five American Negroes speak Black English. At such figures Black English could be nothing less than established vernacular of some age and wide extension, though Dillard also says it is one which was either ignored or not recognized properly until the publications of Stewart in the 1960s.

In one chapter of *Black English* Dillard analyzes the structure of Black English; in another he reconstructs its history. Within the structure of Black English he discovers that Black English does have the basic underlying patterns, peculiar to itself, which a language needs. It has its own syntax, its own system of verbs, its own special way with pronouns, conjunctions, prepositions and relative clauses. It is in its system of verbs, to paraphrase Dillard closely, that Black English reveals its greatest difference from white American, as from white British, dialects, and its most notable resemblance to its own actual ancestors and relatives. To appreciate this difference, and this resemblance, one must recollect that verbs may possess not only tense, but also a property called aspect, *i.e.*, the capacity in a verb which, when utilized, indicates the "ongoing, continuous, or intermittent quality of an action rather than the time of its occurrence."[2] The time of the occurrence of an action, as is well known, is told by tense. To quote Dillard, aspect is "the only obligatory category in the Black English verb system."[3] To quote him further and at some length:

This [*i.e.* the obligatoriness of aspect in the Black English verb] is perhaps [in Black English] the most basic difference from Standard English, since a speaker of Standard English must mark tense but can choose to indicate or to ignore the ongoing or static quality of an action. Black English gives the speaker an option with regard to tense, but its rules demand that he commit himself as to whether the action was continuous or momentary.[4]

The history of Black English Dillard traces back to Africa. Dillard grounds the true ancestor of Black English in the West African Pidgin English often adopted by slaves either in the slave pens before they were taken to the ships or on board the vessels which bore them in chains across the Atlantic. Thus, according to Dillard, Black English began as a language which had no native speakers, for it is important to Dillard that the term *Pidgin* be defined, as he points out that professional linguists do define it, in reference to its lack of native speakers. When Black English did acquire native speakers it was in its second phase, and the speakers tended to be slaves of African

2. *Ibid.*, 43.
3. *Ibid.*, 43–44.
4. *Ibid.*, 44.

extraction who were performing the hard, nasty work of field hands and manual laborers on and around the plantations of the antebellum South. When, again according to Dillard, a language that was Pidgin becomes the only, or the principal, language of a speech community, linguists call that language a Creole. Thus, West African Pidgin English became in America a Creole and, since it was the medium of speech of a community associated with the plantation, a Creole that can very conveniently, in Dillard's creation of labels, be designated as Plantation Creole.

Plantation Creole has not been a language that came and went. Nor was it ever a purely local phenomenon. Wherever they were, the slaves used it and developed it, and in America it has had at least two hundred years of strenuous life. In its third phase—the phase, if I read *Black English* aright, in which it tends now to be found in the big urban ghettos, typically in the North, where the sixth, seventh, and eighth generations of its users tend presently to be congregated—Black English is now undergoing a process which linguists (I am still following Dillard) call decreolization. Under the impact of dynamic forces in the sociopolitical environment current to it now, it is modifying some of its original Pidgin-born peculiarities. In summary, then, as Dillard sees things, Black English is a nationwide phenomenon. Four out of five American Negroes speak it. It is a distinctive language. Its history shows that it began as a Pidgin, became what Dillard calls Plantation Creole, and is now, to a considerable degree, in a stage of decreolization.

The prescription for social action in *Black English* proceeds logically, at least in Dillard's view, from his description of Black English. That prescription has to do with American education. Since so many children speak Black English the sensible course, Dillard says, for American education to adopt is for it not to beat its head against a stone wall. Teachers of black children can, and should, use Black English in the instruction of their children. It should be noted, incidentally, that Dillard does not advocate the exclusive resort to Black English in the formal education of the ghetto child. But he does make crystal clear his conviction that teachers of ghetto children, presumably especially if they are white, handicap themselves in their relations with their charges if they cannot speak Black English. He believes, among other things, that ghetto texts should avail themselves of Black English and cites, in one instance, the three textbooks, *Ollie, Friends,* and *Old Tales,* produced by the Education Study Center in Washington, D.C., of which Stewart is president. These texts, Dillard indicates, present their material in parallel Black English and Standard English versions.

No picture, however, of what Dillard advocates for the ghetto classroom is complete if it tells only of his advocacy of Black English. He feels also that ghetto children should not only hear, and read, their own language in their own classrooms, they should also there have access to their own heroes. They should read not only white writers, but nonwhites like Charles W. Chesnutt or LeRoi Jones, as well as some whites, like William Gilmore Simms, George Washington Cable, and Lafcadio Hearn, who are not presented to American school children as often as they might be. Even so, however, the crucial article to keep in mind about Dillard's prescription for the American school is his insistence that programs for the ghetto school will suffer, and suffer unduly, unless the special knowledge which he thinks he and Stewart have acquired about Black English is put to use in reforming practices and resources in the ghetto school. It is almost literal to say that Dillard advocates Black English as one, if not the prime, official language of the new black classroom.

I have already said that I do not agree with Dillard's major conclusions. I am not, that is, persuaded either that his picture of Black English is reliable or that his sense of what should be done in black classrooms agrees with my own. I admit that much of my reaction to Dillard is personal. He says that four out of every five American Negroes speak his brand of Black English. Incidentally, he also specifies that two populations "formed the groups studied for most of the conclusions drawn within . . . [*Black English*]."[5] One of these "populations" is a "block-long community in an area inhabited almost exclusively by blacks,"[6] and the other was "studied primarily through two nearly bidialetical boys but also through recordings of nearly a dozen youngsters."[7] He does have, he says, "examples taken from most parts of the United States,"[8] but one must suppose that *Black English* does depend overwhelmingly on the data derived from his two main populations, one of them a block of people and the other, almost nothing but two boys. On the other hand, it does need to be emphasized that Dillard's interest in, and contact with, American Negro speech goes far beyond his two population groups. He was born and grew up in West Texas. He has lived and taught and performed research in the eastern United States and in South America and in Puerto Rico. His sense of Negro speech is enriched by experiences of a valuable kind.

But I grew up, as a Negro, in the fairly stable Negro community of Louisville in Kentucky. I believe I knew it well. I entered its public schools in kindergarten in 1914. I taught in its secondary system, in a junior high school for eleven years. I did not leave Louisville until 1945. I was, I believe, the kind of growing boy, young man, and public-school teacher who rubbed shoulders with everybody. Moreover, Negro Louisville, in my days of residence there, was an open community. Class stratifications meant virtually nothing within it. Money certainly did not divide it. Nor did skin color or occupation. I think I heard every variation of Negro speech within it between the day I started to school in 1914 and the day I left Louisville permanently in 1945. And Black English was not the language of Negro Louisville. If you point out that Louisville was small, I will answer that it was not that small. There were always about

5. *Ibid.*, 232.
6. *Ibid.*
7. *Ibid.*, 233.
8. *Ibid.*, 232.

fifty thousand Negroes in it when I knew it. Nor did I stay in Louisville. I went to college, a Negro college, in Ohio. I traveled, and I certainly think I have a pretty good idea of how I expected Negroes to talk wherever I met them, except in the Deep South—upon which I did not trespass at all, but for one brief dash into it, until 1949. I met a sufficient number of Negroes from various walks of life and scattered communities before the middle 1950s, when I went to Louisiana, where local speech is still rather special, to question any announcement that four out of five Negroes speak Dillard's Black English. I speak impressionistically now, but I speak believing I am a qualified witness. Even if I could accept Dillard's thesis about Pidgin English, I cannot accept his percentages. They conflict with my own sense of my own life. They conflict, too, with the speech patterns of ordinary Negroes in the fiction of Negro writers like Langston Hughes, Richard Wright, Ann Petry, Ralph Ellison, John Oliver Killens, James Baldwin, and John A. Williams—authors who write about the Negro world I thought I knew and whose portrayal of Negro speakers confirms, for me at least, the notions I had about such speakers in the transcripts of reality I had filed for ready reference in my own mind. But I am not sold on the Pidgin origins of American Negro speech, either. I am not prepared to dismiss this theory out of hand. I want, however, to put it beside some of the other explanations of Negro speech we have already had. I think we have learned something about Negro speech from them all. And I have had some objections to them all.

But, where Dillard is concerned, it is to his proposed program, far more even than to his theory, that I am most opposed. Why, I ask myself, if white teachers are so smart that they can learn Black English, are ghetto blacks so dumb that they cannot learn their teachers' language? Why, indeed— especially when I recall the emphasis in Dillard's and Stewart's support of Black English on age-grading, which, if I understand it, means that children do tend, in any case, to change their speech as they get older? When a man comes to me telling me that he does not believe that I am inferior, and yet he is ready to take special pains for my benefit so that I need not take special pains in my own behalf, what does that man really think? What, moreover, does he really want? And, putting aside the question of speech, what about the question of ghettos? How does one get rid of them? I suppose we want to get rid of them. I certainly do. I wanted to get rid of them when I was growing up. I want to get rid of them now. All Americans are immigrants, even the Indians, who walked across the Aleutians long ago. Some of the immigrants from Europe had speech problems when they first came over here, and many of them lived in ghettos, too. They got rid of their speech problems and got out of their ghettos, though not necessarily always in that order. And it does not do any good to say that their experience is not relevant to that of Negroes. It is very relevant, except that the Negroes are the only immigrants to America who have been saddled with color caste.

I do not believe that Black English is, or ever has been, an insoluble problem in America. Our unsolved problem — which, incidentally, I believe can be solved — is color caste. And I believe proposals such as those contained in *Black English* take us further from the right solution of that problem. I could, of course, be wrong. For I have lived too long now not to know how fallible are most human notions, even those which we adopt with the best of intentions and which we may think represent the best of information as well as the purest of motives. Even so, this linguists' form of the neighborhood school proposed in *Black English* perturbs me greatly. It fits too well the image of the Great White Father, and it serves too much another perpetuation, under an ostensibly benign impulse, of color caste. I want no part of it, and I say nothing of the vision which rises before me of the new bonanza, if it were adopted, in Black English texts. Wendell Wilkie believed in one world. I do too. I also believe in one America. There will be, thankfully, variety in America, no matter how we try to regiment it. Some of the variety will be heaven-sent. Some of it, no matter what is done or not done, will at least for a long foreseeable future, be associated with the speech of ghetto blacks. That variety, I should like to think, will take care of itself in time. But to take steps to preserve it under the banner of liberal social thought is more than I can countenance or accept. I think the claims of scholarship in *Black English* are excessive, for I do not—I say this slowly and carefully—always agree with the explanations Dillard gives in *Black English* as to why ghetto speakers make certain statements and systematize certain apparent speech habits. And I certainly do not agree with what seems to me to be Dillard's projection of the nature of a national community of American Negro speakers. His scholarship breaks down, it seems to me, at the very vital point where he ceases to deal with sensory data and undertakes to supplement such data with inference. His liberalism breaks down there, too, it seems to me. Whatever he infers for me in Black English is wrong. I think he is wrong, too, about the ghettos. I think they seek a city which he refuses to infer.

The Minstrel Mode

ONE OF *the programs of the Voice of America was of such a nature that these remarks seemed appropriate for it. The whole program was under the supervision of Louis Rubin. It represented an attempt to present, especially for non-Americans, a picture of the comic imagination in American literature.*

Professor Rubin selected critics of American literature who, he thought, should be in the program and suggested topics to these critics for lectures. Finished lectures were taped as read by the critics who prepared them. The tapes thus obtained were, of course, for replay overseas. But the lectures also exist now in the book, published by the Rutgers University Press: Louis D. Rubin, Jr., ed., The Comic Imagination in American Literature.

The late James Weldon Johnson, famed Negro author, is among those who remind us that American minstrelsy did have its origin among the slaves of America's Old South. "Every plantation," in Johnson's words, "had its talented band that could crack Negro jokes, and sing and dance to the accompaniment of the banjo and the bones," so that, again in Johnson's words, "when the wealthy plantation-owner wished to entertain and amuse his guests, he needed only to call for his troupe of black minstrels." Yet Johnson's words do not quite do for us what they should. There were wealthy plantations in the Old South, but never as many as it is easy to suppose. For most of the Old South, like most of Old America, was a frontier. Crude virtues flourished in it. Nor did it cater much to social distance. Its black and white bondsmen, its sturdy yeomen, its new proprietors, as well as its riffraff of every color and description, lived in an atmosphere of easy familiarity. It was in their vulgar fellowship, rather than in the ceremonials of an upper class, that the Negro was first truly marked for his role as an American humorist, the role he played in the minstrel mode.

One should not wonder, then, when Constance Rourke, a closer student of the origins of American humor than James Weldon Johnson, expresses interest in the Negro in the South and the "new Southwest" of Old America. At that early time, of course, Alabama, Mississippi, Louisiana, Arkansas, and even backwoods Kentucky and Tennessee, could be West, Southwest, and new. In all such sections of Old America land was still being cleared. Towns were still being founded. The great highways were still the rivers. Negroes sang and danced on those rivers as they toiled on boats or "labored" around the docks or were being carried in coffles from one auction to another. They sang and danced elsewhere, too, in field and village and in the burgeoning raw cities, like Cincinnati, Louisville, Nashville, and Natchez, or, way down at river's end, New Orleans. From the 1840s and the 1850s Constance Rourke describes a comic trio—the Yankee, the backwoodsman, and the Negro. She deposes that the three tended to merge into a single generic figure of which the long-tailed blue, the costume worn both by Uncle Sam and the blackface minstrel, tended to become, as she points out, a lasting symbol. It was, indeed, as if the Yankee, the backwoodsman, and the Negro were a godsend to people starved not only for the arts of life, but also for the art of living. Each comic figure added a dimension of social nuance, a humanizing influence, to an often otherwise brutelike existence.

This is not to say that there were no plantation minstrels who were black and actually did live on plantations and did perform at a master's whim. Indeed, we still have, hanging in an old mansion in Williamsburg, Virginia, an unsigned painting, dating from around 1790, which shows, as Negro historian of the drama Loften Mitchell describes it, "a group of Negroes near a cabin, watching a banjo player, a drummer and dancers." The painting is entitled *The Old Plant* and clearly is intended to represent black slaves at leisure on a big plantation. These are clearly also slaves who could, if summoned, heed a master's bidding and entertain his guests. But this painting depicts them near one of their own cabins. It emphasizes their private folk behavior. And thus this painting does imply the true genesis of blackface minstrelsy and the American minstrel mode in a genuine folk figure and folk situation.

All over early America, as America moved westward from the Atlantic coast to the banks of the Mississippi and from there onward to America's Pacific slope, this dark-skinned folk figure was much in evidence. It was not only that he was ubiquitous. He was also, even in a society that called itself democratic and prided, even preened, itself on its egalitarianism, somehow separate. As this figure was unique, so was his situation. And, since he was so separate, he could be watched almost as if he were a trophy under glass. Moreover, a certain fascination did attach to watching him. He did have his gifts and his traits—his fiddling, his banjo playing, his tambourine and bones, his melodies, his fables, his tall tales, his dancing that blackface minstrelsy would later characterize as heelology, his general style of life. Constance Rourke quotes a traveler of 1795. "The blacks," said this traveler, "are the great humorists of the nation." They were, indeed, great humorists, and in their humor they were often real, or incipient, minstrels.

The second element in the minstrel mode that requires consideration is impersonation. Apparently the first impersonation of a Negro on an American stage occurred in 1769, before America became a nation, when an English actor, one Lewis Hallam, in Isaac Bickerstaff's comic opera, *The Padlock*, played a drunken Negro on a New York stage. A real Negro, it seems, played the role of Sambo in Murdock's drama,

Triumph of Love, at the Chestnut Street Theatre in Philadelphia
in 1795. Four years later at the Federal Theatre in Boston,
white Gottlieb Graupner, born in Hanover, Germany, and a
claimant to the distinction of being the "father of American
orchestral music," closed the second act of a play by singing
"The Negro Boy." He was encored repeatedly. Other stage
personalities, almost all of them white, in the early years of the
nineteenth century, did Negro bits of one kind or another.
But probably the first impersonation of the Negro which led
directly to blackface minstrelsy must be credited to a young
white man named Thomas Dartmouth Rice.

Rice was born in 1808 in New York City. (Few star blackface
impersonators were not born in the North.) Trained to be a
wood carver, Rice soon gravitated toward the one vocational
world in which he had a permanent interest, the world of the
theater. The end of his teens found him working the towns of
what was then the American West. A sort of theatrical handy-
man, he served as a stage carpenter, a lamplighter, and an
actor in supernumerary roles. In either Cincinnati or, more
probably, Louisville his path crossed that of a Negro hostler
with a hunched-up right shoulder and a rheumatic left leg,
stiff at the knee. From this Negro, Rice borrowed both the
curious dance of a man handicapped by an infirmity, yet still
adroit of movement, and the famous chorus, to which a rash
of versus would eventually be improvised:

> First on de heel tap, den on de toe,
> Ebery time I wheel about I jump Jim Crow.
> Wheel about and turn about and do jis so,
> And ebery time I wheel about I jump Jim Crow.

So it was that Thomas Dartmouth Rice, in blackface, became
"Jim Crow," or "Daddy" Rice, and for the better part of twenty
years, though he was to die paralytic and impoverished, the
sensation of America and England. Late in 1832 he "jumped
Jim Crow" at the Bowery Theatre in New York City. His
ecstatic audience recalled him twenty times. In Washington

he is said to have brought the four-year-old Joseph Jefferson, who would grow up to become one of the eminent actors of the century, onto the stage with him, in blackface and a large sack, to plump the tiny tot out, and then to come down toward the footlights, singing:

> Ladies and Gentlemen, I'd have you for to know
> That I've got a little darkey here that jumps Jim Crow.

In 1836 he took London by storm. Later, he was as enormous a "hit" in Dublin. Perhaps no individual ever matched him as a "single" in Negro impersonation. And Rice, upon occasion, did appear in true blackface minstrel shows. Even so, however, the honor of initiating the true blackface minstrel show is usually accorded to Dan Emmett, composer of "Dixie," and to three other white men: "Billy" Whitlock, banjoist; Frank Bower, expert on the bone castanets; and "Dick" Pelham, owner of a tambourine. Either late in 1842 or early in 1843, as the Virginia Minstrels, this quartet played in New York City the performance out of which the minstrel show was born.

Blackface minstrelsy, as a form of organized theater, lasted a long time. Not until 1928 did the Al G. Field company, the final survivor of hundreds of minstrel troupes, ring down the curtain that rang out the end of professional minstrel shows. It may be difficult now, in the days of technological theater, to realize how successful the living theater of blackface minstrelsy once was. In the years of their prime — which would have been at their very peak in the 1850s and the 1860s — the minstrel shows waxed truly like a green bay tree. They virtually took over as their particular bonanza the big towns, where they for years monopolized the best houses. One company, Bryant's Minstrels, actually played, except for an interruption of nine months in San Francisco, continuously in New York for sixteen years — nine of those years at one spot, Mechanics' Hall. Nor was this company by any means the only minstrel group to stay in one town or one theater for a run of astounding length. There was a time when the minstrel companies, merely in

trying to accede to an authentic popular demand, gave, and
were long forced to continue to give, three performances a
day. They could be found, too, in small towns, in villages,
and in every hinterland. They played on the East Coast, on
the West Coast, in middle America, North and South, overseas
in Europe as far afield as Hawaii and Australia; and we have at
least one account of a band of Hindi minstrels playing and
singing in blackface in nineteenth-century India.

The minstrel show, it is true, did begin as an impersonation
of the southern Negro. It acquired, in addition, a set form.
There was a first part, a second part, and, sometimes, even, a
third part. In the first part the performers sat on stage in a
semicircle, with the interlocutor who played it white and
straight in the middle; Mr. Tambo and Mr. Bones, with their
proper instruments, were at either end. The first part ended
with a walk-around and hoedown. The second part was called
the olio and was really a variety show in which a medley of
acts was presented. It was especially in the olio, which tended
to absorb the occasional third part, that the connection of the
minstrel show with black impersonation first grew thin and
often finally in essence disappeared. The legitimate aspirations
of blackface minstrelsy may be said to have resided in the impersonation of the Negro and the burlesquing of his character.
Burlesquing was important and as legitimate as was impersonation. But the exhibition of virtuosity, *any* virtuosity, and the
inclination of showmen, once they had an audience, to put on
what they regarded as their own best show, supplanted genuine burlesque in blackface minstrelsy with spectacle and stunts.

From their earliest days, for obvious reasons, the minstrel
shows had indulged themselves in street parades. Those
parades grew larger and larger, fancier and fancier, gaudier
and gaudier. So, too, and not only in the olio, did the companies. By 1880 Haverly's Mastodons carried 100 members,
with elaborate stage settings, through America into England,
and beyond. But then another company appeared, with, of
course, 110 members, including "two bands of fourteen

musicians each, a sextette of saxophone players, two drum corps of eight each, two drum majors and a quartette of mounted buglers." Meanwhile, Haverly's Mastodons by the time they arrived, in 1884, at the Drury Lane Theatre in London had added 18 end-men with the traditional tambourines and bones and 6 star end-men who were presented to the audience in relays. And by this date, and later, one might well expect to see in blackface minstrelsy, for they had all appeared there with increasing regularity, bicycle riders, club and hoop manipulators, yodelers, expert whistlers, acrobats, jugglers, contortionists, Chang the Chinese giant, and other sideshow freaks. Arias and episodes from opera were given straight or otherwise, as were a travesty on Sarah Bernhardt known as Sarah Heartburn, animal acts, drill teams, bird and animal imitators, pantomimists and whole plays, sometimes as farces, but (alas!) sometimes as serious attempts at serious art. As early, indeed, as 1845, Monsieur Cassimir, "the Great French Drummer," had regaled New Orleanians with an imitation on his drum of a whole battle in the Mexican war, including not only the firing of small arms and cannon, but all the other sounds of the contending armies. As late as 1928, Al G. Field's company enacted its first part before a skyscraper background in a roof-garden setting. Not even the witty could excuse such a tableau as a cotton field in the clouds.

Gradually and monumentally the Negro and the Negro's true agrarian world had been expunged from blackface minstrelsy. The humor had gone with them. The shows had been converted into extravaganzas, little, if any, different from expensive vaudeville. Once the minstrel songs had been Negro songs dealing with Negro figures: Jim Crow, Zip Coon, Dan Tucker. But, through the years, Dan Tucker had turned white. Zip Coon had sunk into oblivion beneath "Turkey in the Straw." And what was left of both had suffered the same fate as what was left of Jim Crow. It had surrendered to the version of the Negro which had come to constitute the third large element in the minstrel mode.

There was, it is certainly true, never a time, even in early Jamestown, when white Americans did not harbor some special feelings toward people who were black. Thomas Jefferson, for example, is not infrequently cited for his philosophic opposition to slavery. And there can be little doubt but that when Jefferson spoke of freedom for all he meant exactly what he said. Nevertheless, extending justice to Negroes did not also mean to Jefferson the identification of Negroes with Anglo-Saxons. White people, thought Jefferson, were more beautiful than black, more elegantly symmetrical of form. The blacks, however, seemed to him to require less sleep. They were wanting in forethought and much inferior in reason and in imagination. Love, among blacks, in Jefferson's view, was "more an eager desire, than a delicate mixture of sentiment and sensation," and Negroes, as he saw them, could not grieve long, or really be expected to reflect. Apostle of the Enlightenment that Jefferson was, he does, even so, seem conditioned to do his thinking about Negroes along racist lines. It is hardly probable, therefore, that the first whites who impersonated Negroes were not at least a little racist, too.

Nevertheless, the animus against Negroes within America does seem to bear some correlation to the imperial spirit of the plantation South. The more cotton the South grew, both before and after the Civil War, the more it insisted upon an image of the Negro that would fit the Negro for the place in a "plantocracy" where he belonged. Matters were not quite that simple all over America. But they were almost. The pressure of color caste affected not only Negroes. It affected also their representation. And nowhere was their representation a readier tool for racism than in blackface minstrelsy. The little darky who jumped Jim Crow became every Negro — every Negro in real life as well as on the stage.

And so the minstrel mode, in its worst element, invaded American life, in the process reversing a relationship, so that, instead of life dictating to art, art dictated to life. By the days between World War I and World War II, when Al Jolson, in blackface, was singing to his mammy and some Negro actresses were playing that mammy in the movies or on stage, the racist element in the minstrel mode had become, on stage or off, a prescribed cult. It had conquered and, outlasting blackface minstrelsy as such, had put the stamp of its own minstrel mode on virtually every approach of average Americans to Negroes and Negro life.

But this racist stamp could not last and has not. Negroes themselves, using their own accesses to the minstrel mode, long ago began to undermine it. One has but to turn back forty years to the character of Jimboy, Negro vagrant in Langston Hughes's *Not Without Laughter,* to suspect that Negro artists have been deliberately contemptuous of the old orthodoxies in the conventional American minstrel mode. Jimboy himself is a minstrel, a black wanderer who prowls America in search of a decent job, his guitar as his traveling companion, and he sings the blues. W. C. Handy, emerging out of rural Alabama, was to become, after his real life in Memphis and his real pilgrimage to New York, the recognized "Father of the Blues." Both the real W. C. Handy and the unreal Jimboy speak to us of what Charles Keil has called, in his *Urban Blues,* "an expressive male role within urban lower-class Negro culture — that of the contemporary bluesman."

Thus, when Ralph Ellison, in *Invisible Man,* has Tod Clifton "drop out of history" — that is, cease to be his true black self — and so permits Clifton to peddle Sambo, a dancing doll manipulated as a puppet, to street crowds in downtown, white Manhattan, the episode constitutes a perfect metaphor for the racism in the minstrel mode of blackface minstrelsy. Jimboy and W. C. Handy, on the other hand, though not perfect metaphors for a countermovement to this racism, are at least important signposts. For undoubtedly in very actual life the Negro who was once in America's rural South has migrated to the city like, incidentally, both Handy and Jimboy. Undoubtedly, moreover, that Negro has created his own sense of himself. Undoubtedly, finally, he has found, and deputized, his own interpreter of this sense. And that interpreter—Ray Charles, B. B. King, and other artists of their kind and tone— is a bluesman, a black minstrel made by blacks, and, indeed, the latest strain in an American minstrel mode that was always Negro in its origin and largely Negro in its context, but now at last bids fair, with jazzmen and the blues, against the back- ground of an urban scene, to be more Negroid in its creative soul.

Harlem
Renaissance
in the
Twenties

THE ORIGINAL *occasion for this essay was a session of a con-ference at Southern Illinois University on the 1920s in America.*

⊱⊰

I hold that all discussions of the Harlem Renaissance which say too much about Harlem and not enough about the whole of Negro America as it was during the period of the Renaissance should be approached with a considerable amount of wariness. The Renaissance has been transmitted to us largely through its literature. That literature, I believe, in keeping with the Renaissance itself, acquired its substantial character, not from the isolated eccentricities of a place, or from the special programs of a coterie of artists, but rather from its relation to the life and the distinctive temper of an entire nationally extensive community, the American Negro world, as I shall call it, of which, I am firmly persuaded, the Renaissance and everything of consequence attributable to it were ultimately a product and always a faithful and true reflection.

If I am right—if, that is, I judge properly both the written record and the impressions remaining from my own personal recollection—then really to see deeply into this literature of the Harlem Renaissance one is virtually forced to be in adequate possession of a sense of the world out of which the literature came. It will not do to focus one's attention upon Harlem. Between the turn of the century and the end of the Renaissance more than twice as many Negroes poured into Harlem than there are people now in towns like East St. Louis, Roanoke, or Durham. They came from everywhere. The easiest, closest path led straight up the Atlantic coast. It was the most heavily traveled. But a goodly number of black pilgrims filtered in from points of origin scattered across the continent, and some, like Claude McKay and Marcus Garvey, for example, were from the islands of the sea. Harlem did affect all these new-comers. (There is, after all, such a thing as the effect of local custom.) But it did not transform them. The newcomers, the invading host, transformed Harlem. They were freer in New York than they had ever been at any time or place before in their lives. They were also, therefore, if for no other reason, more themselves. They could do their thing. They could be what they had always thought they were. They could roam up and down Lenox and Seventh avenues, and even climb Sugar Hill, and know that they were home. They could not, of course, completely escape the long, intrusive shadow of their white-man boss. They still lived somewhat on his sufferance within an enclave of his all-engulfing larger universe. And it was, moreover, undoubtedly true that Harlem, during the Ren-aissance, did constitute rather deliberately something of a city under glass for white sightseers from the outside — for monied tourists come to see the natives in their native habitat. Its con-sciousness of a white audience was there, even, to a measure, in its serious art. Yet, real as was the influence of white patrons, Renaissance Harlem belonged basically to the world from which its inhabitants came. Those inhabitants were Negroes who had grown up in a Negro world, raised by Negro parents or Negro older relatives, trained in Negro ways, feeling Negro feelings, and thinking Negro thoughts. They could only keep Harlem, in the final analysis, a Negro world, and make of the Harlem Renaissance, in its final analysis, a Negro Renaissance.

It was my own father's generation, possibly the most maligned and, conceivably, the finest in inner discipline and altruistic spirit of any Negro generation that has existed in

America, which in the main did raise and train the Renaissance band of Negroes. And this generation of my parents was the first Negro generation born in freedom.

My grandparents' generation was born in slavery. It could call nothing its own. Among his other deprivations, a slave had absolutely no privacy which he could protect. For obvious reasons his master insisted on the right to know where he was and what he was doing, if it suited the master's interest, every minute of the day and night. Frederick Douglass remembered of his mother that he saw her only three or four times in his entire life and then only late at night. He was a small boy quartered on one plantation. She worked as a field hand on another. To visit him she had to steal away on foot, after a long day's hard physical labor, walk to where he was, and then be sure, unless she was prepared for the lash, to be home, ready to pick up her heavy field-work tools, at the break of day. It is a commonplace of our culture to be sentimental over the relationship between a mother and her offspring. But the system of slavery waxed sentimental over nothing that removed the slave from the direct surveillance of his master or his master's deputy.

Come freedom, however, the status of the Negro changed. Now suddenly it served the purpose of the whites not to have Negroes near, but to have them far, to torture them with social distance so that they would know how abominable and impossible they were. Now these Negroes, who were kept so close during slavery, must be segregated and Jim Crowed. There must even be an etiquette of race relations. For Negroes, never a title of respect. To them, no common courtesies. They must be made to know that they were creatures doomed to live apart, and when the constant insult was not thought to be sufficient, then it was deemed advisable, often by responsible leaders and pillars of the community, that they be terrorized into not forgetting how essential it was for them to live always, metaphorically at least, if not sometimes in literal fact, on their knees. My father's generation, thus, lived in a very private

Negro world. It was in such a world, moreover, that the Renaissance generation achieved maturity. I would dwell on this at length, if I but had the time. For the first distinction of Negro life for decades after freedom was the extreme degree to which it was turned in upon itself. The Negro coming home at night, from working in a white man's world, crossed a great divide. He reentered a private world, shut in from the outside and, in an understandable retaliation, with its own virtually impregnable barriers against the very outsiders whose incivilities had cast it into its general mold. Within this private world, however, the Negro himself roamed, as it were, with exemplary freedom. For this private world was notably compact.

It has never been true that all Negroes look alike, or think alike, or act alike. They do differ. And yet it is salutary sometimes to notice, relatively, how much they do seem to be cut from exactly the same cloth. In spite of talk about the black bourgeoisie, Negroes, certainly until the latest generation, have been practically classless. It would have been for a long time, and may yet be, a most amnesic member of a black elite who presumed that all of his blood kith and kin were similarly elite—just as, moreover, it would have been a truly unique black plebeian who did not have, and know that he had, one or more relatives high in the so-called Negro upper class. The Negro world of the Renaissance was not fragmented by class. Nor was it affected by occupation. Most Negroes, including the professionals who toiled in Negro professions, held Negro jobs. And as this compact world was saved from inner fissures by its lack of great diversities, just so it was bound closely together by the very scarcity of the institutions which served it.

To speak of churches, for example, could give most Negroes almost a sense of intimacy with all other Negroes. Any Negro passing through a strange town who asked another Negro whom he had never seen where the AME church was situated, so long as he said AME and not African Methodist Episcopal, could expect to be understood. For Negroes everywhere were familiar with the several shades of Negro Baptists and the only three Negro Methodist denominations. Negroes knew, too, what kind of Negro businesses to expect in every Negro community. Many Negroes knew the names of just about all the Negro colleges. There were only about a hundred, and the limited number of Negro high schools permitted some of them, like Wendell Phillips in Chicago and Sumner in St. Louis, to be as well known as the best-known seats of Negro higher learning.

There was, too, a Negro press. It was composed of weekly papers, not dailies. But by the time of the Renaissance three Negro weeklies, much as the big television systems of today in our national community, were national institutions of a sort within the Negro world. One of them, the Chicago *Defender,* owned by a man who had been born in Georgia, was virtually the equivalent of a Negro bible. There was something scriptural, too, something like the common voice of the Old Testament prophets, in the zeal with which it preached its gospel of a voluntary Negro exodus from the South. The *Defender* allowed none of its readers to forget how the Negro had suffered solely because he was not white. The lesson, too, was warranted. The Negro world of the Renaissance was not only private and compact, it was also schooled in adversity and misadventure. Not for nothing had it gone through the years from the 1870s until the turn of the century, the years Rayford Logan called the Negro nadir. Negro fortunes in America, indeed, were probably never at a lower ebb than they were in 1900. After all, at the turn of the eighteenth and nineteenth centuries the Negro was legally enslaved. At the turn of the twentieth century he was in theory free.

Yet at that date he was in worse shape than he had been when he was only ten years out of slavery. In 1895 Frederick Douglass had died; and Booker T. Washington, shortly thereafter, at the Cotton States Exposition in Atlanta, had spoken words of good cheer not to the Negro but to the resurgent reactionary South. At all too nearly the same time the Grandfather Clause was meanly contrived and the Plessy-Ferguson

Supreme Court decision was solemnly handed down. Peonage, often camouflaged as cotton tenancy, was rife. The trade of lynching flourished with obscene diligence throughout, especially, the South. The Negro was virtually illiterate. He owned little property. He was generally cut off from the ballot and barred from politics. White churches disdained him. Respectable people shunned him. Even the old abolitionists largely had abandoned him to his own devices. Yet in the thankless climate of the America they knew from McKinley through Wilson, *sans* any flourish of trumpets, the generation of Negroes before the Renaissance was to make, as it were, without straw, the bricks out of which the Renaissance was built, as well as begin the engineering of the rearrangements of Negro opportunity that made possible the Charles Houstons, the Thurgood Marshalls, the Martin Luther Kings, and all the black militants of a later time. This generation did it all under the most adverse of conditions, and it learned techniques and tactics which it imparted to a whole Negro world. It was composed of Negroes who were tempered by their experience of American life, and the quiet virtues they had thereby acquired at tremendous cost they communicated to every Negro of their time, and not least to the class of Negroes younger than themselves who became sensitive enough to play a leading role in the Harlem Renaissance.

One more thing finally they did, one very strange and beautiful thing. Somehow they set the stage, along the way, for a change in the Negro mood. Somehow they ordained a Negro world which by the onset of the Renaissance had taken into itself from somewhere an almost incredible belief in its own special capacity to enjoy life, to treasure vitality for the very sake of vitality. This Negro pride possessed, in its conviction that neither puritanism nor the love of money nor the dominance of science had wrung out of its soul the joy one may get from merely being one's own self, a special sense of its own worth. All over the Negro world in the twenties, incomprehensible as it may seem to people who never knew it, there

was this feeling that Negroes had a special aptitude for living
—merely living—which white people either had never had or
had lost somewhere along the trail to the modern Babylon
which their commerce and their industry was spreading over
the land whose might and granite wonder, in Claude McKay's
famous phrase, were part of the cultural hell testing the
Negro's youth. At Negro gatherings in the twenties the Negro
audience often opened or closed whatever it did with a song
which Negroes call indifferently "The Negro National Anthem"
or "Lift Ev'ry Voice and Sing." With apparently no sense of
incongruity a black assembly of that time would stand upon
its feet and chant with gusto of having its rejoicing rise high as
the listening skies, or making that rejoicing sound as loud as
the rolling seas. And perhaps the curious behavior of those
audiences was justified. If the Negro mood of that day was
apolitical in comparison with the Negro mood of today, it
was also possibly more aesthetic. It did place a premium on
its own version of soul and thus, if possibly at too piteous a
price, assuage the trauma of an outer world's assaults upon
its ego with its own assertion of its superior ability to come to
terms with the problem of humane existence.

Here, then, is a subjective view of that Negro world of which
the Negro Renaissance was part and parcel. It was the world
of *Shuffle Along*, the Negro musical that seemed at the time so
marvellous; the world of Charles Gilpin in *The Emperor Jones;*
of Negro dancers stomping at the Savoy; of the young Louis
Armstrong, descending like a god out of the machine from
high in the flies to the stage of the Lafayette Theater mounted
on a huge golden trumpet; of Marcus Garvey, with his cry of
"Up, You Mighty Race"; of thousands of humble wayfarers,
come, like black voortrekkers, out of the South to seek the end
of their rainbow in the urban environments of the North.

It is also, I wish to argue, the only world in any final terms
which really matters in the interpretation of the literature of
the Negro Renaissance. Prescriptive criticism, I believe, has
little value in the study of what black writers wrote about their

Negro world of almost half a century ago now. Nor is sociological data in its pristine form actually a decided help. Behind
the sociology should be the revealed inner state of mind and
sentiment of a people, the collective consciousness and sub-
consciousness of a world that was neither as articulate nor as
introspective as more sophisticated worlds might have been.

Because I think a grave injustice has been done by those
who dismiss Langston Hughes's sole long piece of fiction
written during the Renaissance as a bad book and an erroneous
attempt at the representation of Negro life, I want to take that
piece of fiction and test it against this world, of which it should
be, if Hughes is any artist at all, actually a revelation and, conceivably, a vindication. I want to put under scrutiny, therefore,
Not Without Laughter. This novel is an account of six years in
the life of a Negro boy named James, or Sandy, Rogers, who
lived, once upon a time, in the town of Stanton, Kansas, a
fictional Kansas town which is really Lawrence, where the
University of Kansas is actually located and where, also,
Langston Hughes spent some of his own youth. Sandy, when
we first meet him, is nine, going on ten. He belongs to a
matriarchal clan headed by his aged but still sturdy grandmother, Hager Williams. Aunt Hager remembers slave times
in Alabama, where she was born. But she has been in Stanton,
in her own words, "fo' nigh on forty years," ever since she and
her husband, now dead these ten years, came up from Montgomery. And in that time, after seeing two boy children die,
she has raised and sent through high school her eldest daughter, Tempy, and educated her second daughter until that
daughter, Annjee, married a yellow Negro, Sandy's father, of
whom Aunt Hager speaks always most disdainfully and with
whom, on those relatively rare occasions when he is around,
she loves to bicker. Her youngest daughter, Harriett, the one
who is giving her her greatest heartache and for whom, perhaps, she has the tenderest regard, is still in high school, but
already rebellious and sullen and wild.

The three daughters are all, like their mother, dark of hue.

But Sandy, a cross between his mother and his father, Jimboy, is brown. Tempy no longer lives under the matriarchal roof. She has wedded well, to Mr. Arkin Siles, a railway mail clerk who owns houses and attends with Tempy, a true Negro *arriviste*, the local black Episcopal church.

On the head of Tempy, convert to the black bourgeoisie, Hughes heaps his withering scorn. This is perhaps the novel's philosophically most questionable motif, though understandable as an overreaction from a Negro author like Hughes, whose identification with the Negro masses certainly seemed genuine enough, but who was himself, nevertheless, the nephew of a Negro Congressman (from whom, indeed, he got his Christian name of Langston) and the grandson of a woman whose first husband had been one of the free Negroes who accompanied John Brown to Harper's Ferry. Around the figures of Annjee, however, and of adolescent Harriett, Hughes weaves a parable that lifts Gunnar Myrdal's famous dichotomy of Negro leadership—the School of Accommodation versus the School of Protest—out of the cold, forbidding world of academic jargon and scholarly demonstration and, passing it through the sea change of his art, reincarnates it in the living flesh of the two girls. Annjee is strong-bodied and placid, full of love for her handsome yellow husband and of grateful wonder that he has found her acceptable as a wife, proud and considerate of her son, and, as she once points out, one of the few colored girls in Stanton of a sufficiently equable disposition to have spent, as she has, five years working in the kitchen of the white, and constitutionally querulous Mrs. J. J. Rice. Harriett, at sixteen, is a slim black beauty, with a satiny skin, a talent for song and dance, and a growing bitterness, which she finds it hard to contain, against both white oppression and Negro toleration of the same. Aunt Hager in her dreams, it would seem, has reconciled the two. She wants Sandy to grow up to be as great as Booker T. Washington *and* Frederick Douglass and to emulate them both. She takes in washings and holds, as best she can, her family

together against that day when Sandy will be a man and will
have brought honor to himself and credit to his race.

It is this dream of Aunt Hager, really, which sets the tone
and dominates the form of the panoramic view of a Negro
family, seen through the ingénu eyes of a boy coming to
maturity, which is what the novel actually is. That this should
be so has seemed greatly to trouble some critics who apparently believe that only accounts like *Native Son* and *Invisible Man,* in which Negroes are futilely angry all of the time
and ignominiously defeated in the end, or misty excursions
into the poetry of the ineffable such as *Go Tell It On the Mountain,* are honest and worthwhile expressions by Negro writers
of the nature of Negro life. *Native Son, Invisible Man, Go Tell
It On the Mountain* deserve all the accolades that can be con-
ferred upon them. They are good books, which tell in memorable ways part of the truth. But they do tell only *part.* To
some degree, indeed, they have perpetrated a literary fallacy.
Negroes have had their problems in America. Who would dare
say otherwise? And the millennium of social justice in America is still, apparently, far in the distant future.

And yet, when we look unblinkingly at the facts, the real
story of the Negro in America is the story of his success.
Against great odds he has not failed. The admission that he
has not seems to displease many people, some of them white,
others of them, unfortunately, colored. But the black American
has never been destined for catastrophe. He has been destined for success. Biological failures die. There are five times
as many Negroes in America today as there were when President Lincoln signed the Emancipation Proclamation. The
Negro has been, when defined in efficient rather than conventional terms, a sociological success. As the years advance
and the Negro's horizon of opportunity widens he is translat-
ing his ability to survive and to live with himself and others
into forms of political and economic activity which, even in the
standardized terms of our American system, can be recognized
as success. It is quite possible, then, for a Negro family to be

as poor as the family in which Sandy grows up, to have its differences—the differences that take Tempy to Mr. Siles, Annjee to Jimboy, and Harriett through a flight from home and a fling at prostitution into top billing in the show world as a queen of the blues—to be limited in its resources, lacking in its connections with the powerful and the affluent, void of a so-called distinguished ancestry, and dependent only upon its inner will and strengths, and yet, like Sandy's family, to be a rich haven for the human spirit and a place of nurture for very decent human beings.

In *Not Without Laughter*, Langston Hughes, to his eternal credit, faces up to this so-far eternal verity of the Negro's existence in America. He goes into the private world of the Williams family, itself as compact as the Negro world from which it takes its character. In that world he finds adversity. But he also finds the strength to meet mischance. And, above all, he finds an ability to sustain a love of life itself. He finds it in Jimboy. He finds it in Annjee. He finds it in Harriett. He finds it being steadily inculcated in young Sandy. He finds it in the Negroes who file in and out of the four-room frame dwelling on Cypress Street, an alley really, where the Williamses live. He belabors its modification and abasement in Tempy, who has, after all, been corrupted by white ideals. But at the very end of the novel he finds it transported into the new promised land of the North, both in the crowd at the theater on the South Side which applauds Harriett and her fellow entertainers (and even joins them in their routines when, as is not too infrequent, it is so minded) and in the strains of the spiritual Sandy hears on his way home from the show with Annjee—the spiritual that is drifting out into the night of a black ghetto in the urban North, lifted onto the vehicle of a passing wind by old black southern voices singing in a northern store, which their possession of the voices has made into a black southern church.

The people who find unpalatable Langston Hughes's gospel, who prate of his shirking his responsibilities as a social seer to his black constituency, also disapprove of his lack of skill and power as an artist. *Not Without Laughter* is not a pretentious work of art. It is not stuffed with elaborate esoterica that require even more elaborate interpretation, so that both an author and a critic can participate in a precious game which permits their vanities to realize how superior they are to a common reader. It tells its story simply but intelligently. It is a family chronicle as well as, in effect, a voyage from boyhood to the threshold of maturity. It integrates two pictures into one illuminating revelation of the inside of Negro life. And so it is put together like the joint portrait it is supposed to be, not like a play. It is about Negroes and it is full of softly slurred and very convincingly reproduced Negro speech. But it also takes a lesson from *Huck Finn.* Its style is in itself a subtle reproduction of a Negro idiom. It is, this style, in its own way, a Negro world.

Not Without Laughter has its faults. The novel contains its share of interpolated tales, although those tales seem to me no more extraneous than the interpolated tales in *Tom Jones* or *Joseph Andrews.* The novel also has more than its share of overly sentimental moments. But none of these faults obtrude on the novel's first great virtue. This novel is a tale so well told that it does achieve the impression of making the real world live within its pages.

Hughes's imagination must have worked at a level of creativity which lesser mortals never know when he created this book. At the beginning of the story a cyclone strikes the Williams' house, wrenching away and bearing into oblivion the Williams' porch, which then must be replaced. Far down into the novel, Sandy wants a sled for Christmas. But his mother has been sick and temporarily laid off from work. Moreover, at this very juncture, Harriett gets stranded in Memphis where she has abandoned the carnival with which she ran away from home. And so one night Sandy sees his mother, who has dragged herself from bed, out behind the house poking in the scraps of wood left by the carpenters who replaced the porch. He knows then that he will not get his sled, and we recognize the strange inconsequence of life—the porch and the sled and the carnival, chance and human passion, and uniting all, in this novel, the talent of an artist who could remember a miniscule effect such as the debris from a cyclone's aftermath.

In *Not Without Laughter*, Hughes's creative powers operate at such a level not once, but constantly. They operate, moreover, in this fashion, not only in the realm of incident, but also in the business of character revelation. One of the big speeches in the book, if not the biggest, is put into the mouth of Jimboy, Sandy's father. He is upbraiding Sandy for buying candy with the coppers Aunt Hager has entrusted to the boy for Sunday School. "To take money and use it for what it ain't s'posed to be used is stealing," Jimboy says. And he adds, "That's what you done today, and then come home and lie about it. Nobody's ugly as a liar, you know that! . . . I'm not much maybe. Don't mean to say I am. I won't work a lot, but what I do, I do honest. White folks get rich lyin' and stealin'—and some niggers gets rich that way, too—but I don't need money if I got to get it dishonest, with a lot of lies trailing behind me, and can't look folks in the face. It makes you feel dirty! It's no good! . . . Don't I give you nickels for candy whenever you want 'em?" Clearly Jimboy's speech is aimed not only at Sandy, but at posterity. It utters an ethical judgment on the civilization which today has gone to the moon as well as to places nearer home which I need not name. It also reflects on everything I have tried to say about the Harlem Renaissance and the Negro world which, I have argued, bred the Renaissance and determined what the Renaissance would be. Such speeches always court the danger of seeming contrived, of not really appearing to belong in the text if the text is supposed to be part of a story that really happened and not merely a sermon or a tract. And perhaps the sense of a little touch of contrivance may attach itself to Jimboy's lecture. But, if it does, as is probably the case, it is still only a very little touch. For the speech is part of a situation that has come alive for us, and it does come as a logical expression from Sandy's father at the time he makes it. Above all, we have come to know Jimboy. He is a black sheep.

But he is not one of Dante's cold-blooded sinners. Nor is he an idiot. In fact, he is, within his limits, the very kind of person in "real life" who should say what he does when he does and precisely as he does.

The speech is in character for him, just as the Hughes novel is in character for the Renaissance. It is a fable of Negro life in America. It is not a bauble to attract the tourist trade. The Renaissance, the customary legend goes, lasted for less than fifteen years, and then was swept away by the depression. I prefer to believe that it only disappeared for a while beneath a rush of events that concealed its form and may have even diluted its content. But it is a theory of mine that in black America a cumulative process is perennially at work. The Bigger Thomases may come and go. The Williams families, in black America, constitute the equivalent of an eternal verity. They are always there, ready when one New Negro has run his course, to produce another, to denounce, like Jimboy, meanness and duplicity, and to work like Aunt Hager and her children, if in various ways, still with a concerted aim, for a better world, for all the Williamses, of every color and every breed, not only "by and by," but here and now, and in an America, indeed, which the Williamses will have helped to make more what every Williams of good will and bright vision would have it be.

The Ghetto
of the Negro Novel:
A Theme with
Variations

*"THE GHETTO of the Negro Novel: A Theme with Variations"
is an essay I prepared as my lecture when I was one of the six Distinguished Lecturers for the National Council of Teachers of English
in 1970 and 1971. It is an obvious updating, which I believed the
times warranted, of my original remarks on the ghetto of the Negro
novel almost twenty years earlier.*

*This lecture was published, with those of the five other lecturers
whose incumbency as Distinguished Lecturers coincided with mine,
in* The Discovery of English: NCTE 1971 Distinguished
Lectures.

>≡<

In these days when more than a million and a half Negroes live
in the five boroughs of New York City and another million on
the South Side and elsewhere in Chicago, as well as scattered
millions more in places like Watts and Hough, or even in
Atlanta or New Orleans, it may be difficult to realize what the
typical Negro has actually been for most of the time he has
spent as an adornment of the American scene. What he has
actually been is a figure of earth, not a denizen of the city
streets. Until the Civil War he worked on a southern plantation or in some job connected with a staple-crop economy
dominated by the felt needs and the ethos of the class that is
often called the planters of the Old South. After the war he
got emancipated from the legal status of chattel slavery. He

did not get emancipated from his southern home. His life went on far too much as it had been before the adoption of the Thirteenth, Fourteenth and Fifteenth Amendments. He still lived in, or near, fields which were the theater of his daily toil. He was still largely the hapless victim of some white-man boss. And when he lifted up his eyes to contemplate the horizons surrounding him, he could still see only southern sights, still hear only southern sounds, and still find the farthest ranges of his physical universe only in the astronomy of a southern sky.

Statistical data confirm, and document, the southern agrarianism of the Negro throughout by far the greater part of his American existence. In 1870, at the first census after the Civil War, 92 percent of all the Negroes in America (I have somewhat rounded off all the figures which will follow), 4,420,000 out of a total of 4,880,000, lived in the South, a South that was not composed primarily of towns. Thirty years, about a generation, later, at the turn of the twentieth century, out of 8,830,000 Negroes—almost twice as many, incidentally, as in 1870—7,920,000, or 89 percent of the total, still lived in a South where they were still largely adjuncts of the southern soil. Indeed, as late as 1930, even after the passage of another thirty years and the coming of another generation, 9,360,000, or 78 percent, of 11,890,000 American Negroes, still had not left the South and still, in most of their personal careers, were repeating much of the pattern of existence of their parents and grandparents and great-grandparents.

Yet, when one turns from Negro life to Negro literature, and especially to the Negro novel, one may well experience almost immediately the shock of a sharp and powerfully arresting recognition. The Negro novel is a city novel. It almost always has been. It is not that the Negro novel lacks absolutely any connections with the rural South. But the contrast in it of its prevailing setting with the most apparent fact of Negro location in America is almost incredibly enormous. The southern agrarian setting does not even begin to appear in the Negro novel in any degree or to any extent commensurate with its actual, and, for a long time, virtually ubiquitous involvement with Negro life. The first Negro novel, *Clotel* (1853), concentrates as much on Richmond and New Orleans, and Washington, as it does on rural Mississippi. The second Negro novel, *The Garies and Their Friends* (1857), establishes the major portion of its action in Philadelphia. And all of the big Negro novels—big in terms both of their reputation and their influence—like *Native Son* and *Invisible Man,* easily the two biggest of them all, tend either to be set within an urban ghetto or shaped and controlled by the culture of the town.

What accounts for this anomaly? Why are the memorable scenes of the Negro novel set in urban ghettos? Why are not these same scenes drenched instead with the physical atmosphere of the land of cotton, the rhythms of growing seasons in subtropical climes, the images of hoe hands and roustabouts and of Negroes walking down some lonesome southern road? What must we know, or, at least, suspect, about Negroes, about their inner thoughts and their private lives, to understand what well may be the meaning of the Negro novel's obvious predilection for the Negro ghetto and its apparently interrelated aversion to the southern agrarian scene?

There is, of course, no certain answer. But it may help to recollect the old-time darky, with whom the white folks were themselves so ecstatically enamored. He was, in provenience, a plantation Negro. And he represented everything that Negroes, given the freedom to express their unvarnished thoughts, viewed as the opposite of all of the ideas about themselves of which they approved. Happy-go-lucky, as docile as a child, uneducable, insensitive to slight and injury—this Negro satisfied the white man's fond hypothesis that Negroes were born to be enslaved. With the demise of slavery, therefore, this Negro belonged, for his own good as well as in the best interests of the state, within the strict confines of color caste. This Negro must never be permitted to think himself as good as any white man. ("Would you want your daughter to marry one of them?") And so the "good" white man perpetuated, if not his plantation, at least his plantation legend. In song and story, as well as in the picture of God's universe which was instilled into every properly bred white child before that child could read or write, he kept alive the image of the right kind of Negro, the kind who knew his place and stayed therein, whose head, like Old Black Joe's, was always bending low, and whose native habitat, as divine fiat had made it clear, was beneath the foot of every white man in that hierarchy of law and custom of which segregation was the keystone and discrimination the breath of life.

A libelous fraud was what Negroes called this darky. So much of him offended them that they could reconcile themselves to no attribute associated with him. Among other things, as we have seen, he lived in the agrarian South. Negro novelists, consequently, have tended to leave him there. Their Negro— the Negro of their very real subjective fact rather than of the white supremacist's self-hypnotic, autistic thought—has been too hostile to the white man's racial creed to bask in the sunshine of any white man's supposedly seraphic South. And so, if it has served no other function, the ghetto of the Negro novel has served the Negro novelist as an objective correlative for his disdain of the pretensions of color caste. Set this ghetto against the grinning darkies in blackface minstrelsy or the groveling black servitors of literature like "Marse Chan" and one has a physical setting which announces its dissent from the standard preferences of the cult of white skins *uber Alles*. Surely as much as anyone the Negro novelist knows where Negroes have actually had their homes. Surely, too, he could have placed those homes in his fiction to correspond with actuality, in the rural South (just as, incidentally, he could have made his characters talk like Brer Rabbit or cut the fool like Stepin Fetchit). That he chose the ghetto as his symbol, rather than the plantation, is a deliberate act of some significance. It is probably also a most eloquent indication of his basic attitudes toward color caste, and a strong suggestion that he shares, or feels he shares, those attitudes essentially with all Negroes.

If, however, the ghetto of the Negro novel is thus the kind of dual revelation that it well may be, it is also, then, conceivably an entree into, not merely the consciousness of a group of artists, but also the collective consciousness of Negroes as a cohesive whole. One must thus assume, if only from the persistence of the ghetto in the Negro novel, a similar persistence among Negroes of disaffection with the plantation legend, as with the entire body of behavior and belief which that legend was created to make seem true. This disaffection constitutes a theme, an underlying diapason in perennial black reaction to the white man's world, which seems exempt from change. But themes, in life and literature, as in music, may be exposed to variation, without destruction of their fundamental character. The ghetto of the Negro novel is a theme that does retain its fundamental character. Always it speaks of how very much Negroes resent the indignities America has forced upon them. Always it whispers, as it were, the words of Cinquez in one of the *Amistad* trials, "Give us free. Give us free." [1] Always it calls for the end of one era of American life and the beginning of a genuine new day. But it has done this now for well over three generations. And it has become a theme with variations. As time has passed, indeed, it has never varied in its basic composition. But it has elaborated upon that basic composition in ways that have in themselves been varied. It has thereby afforded us a picture of the Negro mind which reflects both a permanent cast of Negro thought and the sensitivity of that cast to changes in the Negro's immediate environment.

Before the Harlem Renaissance, the ghetto of the Negro novel was largely an explication of Negro resourcefulness in adjusting to a culture aggressively intolerant of Negroes. The years of this ghetto were, indeed, the years when Negroes had little choice except to attempt mere brute survival, on terms acceptable to the dominant whites. The shape of the early ghetto of the Negro novel did acquire, then, to a great extent

1. William A. Owens, *Slave Mutiny: The Revolt on the Schooner Amistad* (New York, 1953), 234.

the shape of the Negro experience of life immediately pertaining to it. But with the Renaissance an external environment changed. The Renaissance itself celebrated an entity which it called the New Negro. This New Negro was a creature of hope and pride, an emblem of a race now not only able to survive, but also to boast of an innate capacity for going beyond brute survival to the enjoyment, on terms supplied by itself, of the good things of life. And so the ghetto of the Negro novel of the Harlem Renaissance is the ghetto on a buoyant note. Wrong as has been color caste, bad as have been its ravages on Negro life, says this ghetto, they have hurt the Negro less than the scramble for gain and the repression of natural desires have dehumanized the American white. Inviolate against the Philistines and Babbitts, the Negro, it continues, has preserved his link with the world of healthy instinct. A familiar strain in the novel of the Renaissance is the Negro who passes for white and then returns, a pilgrim from whose eyes the scales have fallen, to his own people. For joy, like the innocence of a good weekend romp at the Savoy, flourished in the ghetto of the Renaissance.

The urban North was then not only an escape. It was the promised land. Like a country at the end of a rainbow, it was where Negroes, at last, could really be themselves. The South had inhibited them. And it had also kept close watch over them. In the South the "paterollers" were always there, seeing to it that Negroes did not get "uppity," and also seeing to it that Negroes never forgot that they were living in a white folks' world. How different, however, was the northern Negro ghetto. It brought together a throng of Negroes who, from their very density, gained anonymity as well as a fraternal communion with each other. And so in the ghetto, away from the white folks' prying eyes and the example of the white folks' enervating ways, Negroes could talk Negro talk, laugh Negro laughter, indulge themselves in Negro ways of having Negro fun, and yet, in their serious moments, of which their self-controlled ghetto existence was far from entirely bereft, contribute to a common Negro conception of a better social order and join with other Negroes in efforts to make that conception, after all, come true.

Not for nothing, hence, did the titles of some novels of the Renaissance read as they do: *Home to Harlem, One Way to Heaven, The Walls of Jericho, Dark Princess, God Sends Sunday, Not Without Laughter.* The Negro novel of the Renaissance is, of course, not all of one piece. Sometimes it satirizes Negroes. Sometimes it pillories them. Its ghetto, too, has its sordid and forbidding aspects. Yet, even so, its ghetto is remarkably consistent in its proclamation both that Negroes are fine people and that in their new homes in the urban North they will build a New Jerusalem. The final scene of Langston Hughes's novel of the Renaissance, *Not Without Laughter,* occurs on a Chicago street. A summer night has softened the harsh daytime contours of Chicago's South Side. Sandy, the boy who approaches manhood in the novel, is walking home with his mother. Neither of them is Chicago-born, and both of them already know that the Chicago ghetto is far from perfect. But somewhere near them, in a small storefront church, a little band of black worshippers, in soft southern speech, is singing an old Negro spiritual, "By and By." This is the ghetto of the Harlem Renaissance.

That variation of the ghetto, however, apparently was not to last, nor was the Negro mood which gave every evidence of sustaining it. The Harlem Renaissance was a phenomenon of the 1920s. In America the 1920s were followed by a Great Depression. Nowhere in America during the depression were soaring spirits the order of the day. In ghetto after northern ghetto, in "real life," Negroes, many of them migrants from the South, were discovering the shortcomings of the promised land. Out of that discovery, moreover, emanated the variation in the novelistic ghetto which may be found, among other places, in Richard Wright's masterpiece, *Native Son,* the ghetto which is almost surely the ghetto of the Negro novel in its classic form and which, in great likelihood, is nearer still to that form in Ann Petry's 1946 edition of *The Street* than in the *Native Son* to which *The Street* had over five years to assimilate itself. The ghetto of *Native Son* creates monsters. The message it conveys inheres not simply in the violence of its protagonist when he smothers to death, ostensibly by accident, white Mary Dalton. It is contained as deeply in the romantic aspirations of this protagonist and a black confidante of his when, idling along on a Chicago street, they play-act at being white. And it finally comes home full force in the play, not the novel, *A Raisin in the Sun,* when Lena Younger, using her recently deceased husband's life insurance (an irony that should not go unnoted), begins to purchase for her family a house in white Clybourne Park, outside the ghetto, where her grandson may grow up free from the ghetto's effect of slow assassination on its occupants.

The ghetto of the Negro novel of the age of Wright was the ghetto of unqualified integration. It marked the manner in which the ghetto as an exciting new frontier, the ghetto of the Harlem Renaissance, had turned into the ghetto of a city of dreadful night, the ghetto of *The Street.* And then it counseled what to do. It admonished escape. But that variation of the ghetto now also has had its day. To some extent it has been re-placed by an act of retrogression, a return to the New Negro of the Harlem Renaissance with his accent on the hypothesis that black is beautiful. To some extent, also, it is as aghast as was the age of Wright at the chamber of horrors which the original ghetto has turned out to be. But it has rewritten the prescriptive portion of its script. Whether or not its ghetto is as nasty as some novelistic Negro ghettos have been, this ghetto is a citadel to be defended, not a disaster to be abandoned. It is in the role, then, of the ultimate in race patriots, the fighter to the bitter end, that the black narrator-protagonist of John A. Williams' *The Man Who Cried I Am* relays back across the Atlantic to a black separatist in America the contents of King Alfred, the contingency plan of the government of the United States for the elimination, if need be, of all the blacks within its borders — "elimination" here, it should be carefully observed, having all the Nazi-atrocity connotations of Belsen, Buchenwald and Dachau. It is in keeping, moreover, with a world so dichotomized that not only this narrator-protagonist and the black separatist to whom he talks, but also the hitherto unsuspecting, white-looking black collaborator, a tool for espionage of the whites, who stumbles on a transcription of the relay, should all be destroyed by the lily-white technicians of the CIA, or some organization like it. For the narrator-protagonist's death and that of the black leader to whom he has communicated King Alfred, as well as, very especially, that of the black collaborator, do all but illustrate one sound conclusion: the futility of trying to do business with the white man, the implacability of color caste, and the stern necessity for all blacks to realize how, only with their own kind, can they find trust and brotherhood, beauty and life, love, honor, and respect, and peace—the peace that whites will allow only to nonwhites who servilely submit to white supremacy.

A theme with four variations is what the ghetto of the Negro novel may well have been over the last seventy years. This theme with its four variations may well represent also, with fair precision, the states of the Negro mind over that same period. Does anything other than a basic aversion to color caste underlie these variations and, if it does, is it present both in the ghetto of the novels and in the mind of the Negro people, whom obviously the ghetto and all Negro literature purport, and hope, to represent? I think it does. I think it is, and let me now, in closing, and in attempting to justify what I assert, attempt also to speak, in my own person, as plainly and as simply as I can.

I believe that all the variations on the basic theme in the ghetto of the Negro novel speak with a common voice whose modulations of any kind are more apparent than real. I believe that all these variations demonstrate a constantly more comprehensive awareness on the part of Negroes in America of the true nature of American color caste and a constantly increasing willingness on their part to accept the proposition that

Negroes, if they wish to live in America at all, can reconcile themselves to no compromise with color caste, for, in color caste, there is, ultimately, no compromise with Negroes. The indispensable requirement of color caste is, of course, precisely what the words imply. All the members of the caste must be kept within the caste. Then, as those without, and presumably always above, the caste must agree, all the members of the caste may always be dealt with as if they were all made from one mould. If such a disposition seems a travesty upon democracy, it is. But it is also a perversion of any genuine belief in the value of humanity. Black separatism at the moment is the modish variation of the Negro novelist's black ghetto. I do not believe in black separatism any more than I believe in color caste. Nor do I believe that either represents a final phase of black-and-white relations in America. On the other hand we can learn, I do believe, from the progression of mutation in the variations on the theme of the ghetto in the Negro novel. And what I think we learn is how expensive a luxury color caste is for whites. If they must have it, I suppose they must. But surely the more they have of it, the less they may ever have of anything really worth the trouble of continuing to exist in a world where the only value without price is the value of humanity.

Jean Toomer's
Cane: An Issue
of Genre

THE GREAT *upsurge of interest in Negro literature which has accompanied recent attention to American minorities has had as one of its focal points an appreciation of the merits of Jean Toomer's* Cane. Cane *is an unusual work of art. The sheer beauty of much of it captivates many of those who read it. It contains poetry and prose. And in either Toomer in* Cane *expresses an exquisite lyric sensibility.*

Even so, Cane *is now a source of some anguish to most older Negro critics of Negro literature. It can hardly be argued that they undervalue* Cane. *But the present esteem of* Cane *tends not to be based on terms which reflect their way of seeing it. Moreover, in that very circumstance they can read a signal instance of their failure to command the wide audience they have always wanted.*

"Jean Toomer's Cane: *An Issue of Genre" was first presented as a paper before a section of an annual meeting of the South Atlantic Modern Language Association in Atlanta.*

⋝⋨

It may well be that the biggest thing there is at the moment in black studies and certainly in Negro literature is Jean Toomer's *Cane*.[1] Interest in it seems to be at a fever pitch. And part of the interest radiates around what can be referred to as a question of identity. Some call *Cane* a novel. Some do not. The some who do not, incidentally, tend to belong to the now elder generation of Negro students of Negro literature.

1. Jean Toomer, *Cane* (New York, 1923).

Cane was published as a book first in 1923. It is important to note that a goodly measure, if not all, of it had appeared in separate autonomous bits before the appearance of the book. Arna Bontemps, for example, in his introduction to a paperback *Cane* issued in 1969, cites *Broom, Crisis, Double Dealer, Liberator, Little Review, Modern Review, Nomad, Prairie,* and *S4N* as periodicals in which parts of *Cane* appeared before the appearance of the whole.[2] When *Cane* did appear, in 1923, it was organized in three sections—each section, as well as the whole book, to paraphrase an apt observation of Bontemps, constituting a melange of poetry and prose whipped together in what Bontemps calls explicitly a "kind of frappe."[3] In the first section there are six short stories or sketches in prose and twenty interpolations of verse of varyings lengths and probably representing fourteen separate poems. In the second section there are seven short stories or sketches in prose and nine interpolations of verse representing, apparently, seven separate poems. In the third section there is one story only, the novelette "Kabnis," presented much in the form of a play —the form in which it had been offered for the stage and there rejected, by Kenneth MacGowan, for lack of plot—and five interpolations of verse, three of them repetitions of the same one-stanza poem and the fourth, a quotation of a portion of a Negro spiritual. The stories in the first section are all set in Georgia and associated with the variety of small-town life which is more agrarian than urban. In the second section the setting shifts to Washington and, in one story, called "Bona and Paul," to Chicago. Georgia, its countryside and small towns, is again the setting in "Kabnis," the third section. Clearly it is possible to find a certain unity, or certain unities, of setting in *Cane*. No single character, however, or group of characters, appears in more than one story or sketch.

Cane was reviewed in the two important Negro journals and house-organs, *Opportunity,* of the National Urban League, and

2. Cf. Jean Toomer, *Cane,* with an introduction by Arna Bontemps (New York, 1969), vii. This is a Perennial Classic paperback.
3. *Ibid.,* x.

Crisis of the NAACP, shortly after its publication. The review in *Opportunity* appeared in December of 1923; [4] that in *Crisis*, in February of 1924.[5] The reviewer for *Opportunity* was Montgomery Gregory, then Director of Dramatic Art and Professor of Public Speaking at Howard University. The reviewer for *Crisis* was its founder and editor, W. E. B. DuBois, whose heroic stature in the history of the American Negro needs here no proclamation. DuBois had little, if anything, to say about the form of *Cane*, except to call it, unequivocally and without hesitancy, a book of stories and poems. He was, as a matter of fact, much more interested in disputing Toomer's knowledge of Georgia, where Toomer had lived for four months and DuBois for thirteen years. He was also interested in recognizing Toomer's knowledge of human beings. Montgomery Gregory, on the other hand, examined the form of *Cane* in some detail. Without ever labeling *Cane* a novel, but with evident indebtedness to the foreword supplied for *Cane* by Waldo Frank, Gregory did find in the book verse, fiction, and drama "fused into a spiritual unity, an 'anesthetic equivalent,' [Waldo Frank's own words in direct quotation] of the Southland."[6] Yet a check word by word of Gregory's review will disclose that Gregory was able to sense this spiritual unity without ever alluding to *Cane* as a novel, and the reference to Toomer in an account of an *Opportunity* dinner for writers, given in 1925, is to "Jean Toomer, Poet and Short Story writer, author of 'Cane.'"[7] In *The Negro Caravan*, an anthology first published in 1941 and edited by three Negro scholars highly venerated by their contemporary, and even younger, black colleagues, Sterling Brown, Arthur Davis, and the late Ulysses Lee, *Cane* is a "collection of sketches short stories, and poems."[8] In *Dark Symphony*, an anthology of Negro literature first published as

4. Montgomery Gregory, "Our Book Shelf," *Opportunity*, I (December, 1923), 374–75.
5. W. E. B. DuBois and Alain Locke, "The Younger Literary Movement," *Crisis*, XXVII (February, 1924), 161.
6. Gregory, "Our Book Shelf," 374.
7. "The Opportunity Dinner," *Opportunity*, III (June, 1925), 177.
8. Sterling Brown, Arthur Davis, and Ulysses Lee (comp.), *The Negro Caravan* (New York, 1941), 41.

recently as 1968, with one black editor, James A. Emanuel, and one white, Theodore L. Gross, *Cane* is a "miscellany of Toomer's early work, containing fictional portraits and poems of life in the villages of Georgia and in Washington, D.C." [9] It is virtually that, also, incidentally, in *Black Voices*, edited by Abraham Chapman,[10] an older white scholar whose attachment to Negro literature may be much conditioned by the close personal relations he once had with Richard Wright as well as by his sympathetic reading of the older Negro scholars. Quite possibly, the consensus on *Cane*, as its form did appear to Negro scholars of the older generation, does affirm itself loudly and clearly in *Negro Voices in American Fiction*, published at Chapel Hill in 1948, and written by Hugh Gloster, now the president of Morehouse College, but for most of his professional life a professor or department head of English at various Negro colleges and, additionally, the founder and first president of the College Language Association, once, if not still, the Negro facsimile of MLA. In *Negro Voices in American Fiction* Gloster classifies *Cane* as "a potpourri of stories, sketches, poetry, and drama." [11] One deviation from this probable consensus may here be observed. Alain Locke, a Negro scholar of great authority among Negroes, and some whites, in his day, and a catalyst of such power and magnitude in the Harlem Renaissance as sometimes to be called its midwife, in the "Who's Who of the Contributors" to *The New Negro,* a volume prominently associated with the Harlem Renaissance (originally a special issue of *Survey Graphic*) which Locke edited, specifically, but rather cursorily, refers to Toomer as the author of *Cane*, "a novel." [12]

It is highly conceivable that the current disposition to call *Cane* a novel may have derived much, if not all, of its original impetus from a passage in Robert Bone's now relatively well-

9. James A. Emanuel and Theodore L. Gross (comp.), *Dark Symphony* (New York, 1968), 97.

10. Abraham Chapman (ed.), *Black Voices* (New York, 1968).

11. Hugh Gloster, *Negro Voices in American Fiction* (Chapel Hill, 1948), 128.

12. Alain Locke (ed.), *The New Negro* (New York, 1925), 145.

known *The Negro Novel in America,* first published in 1958. Gloster wrote of Negro *fiction,* all of Negro fiction; Bone, only of the Negro novel. Darwin Turner has said of *Cane,* "It is not a novel, not even the experimental novel for which Bone pled to justify including it in his study of novels by Negroes." [13] He could have quoted Bone: "Jean Toomer's *Cane* (1923) is an important American novel. By far the most impressive product of the Negro Renaissance, it ranks with Richard Wright's *Native Son* and Ralph Ellison's *Invisible Man* as a measure of the Negro novelist's highest achievement." [14] For, whatever Bone's inducements in dealing with *Cane,* he did nothing by halves. If he made *Cane* a novel—which, of course, it may be— he also made it a good one, which, of course, it may be also. And yet, in the light of most that had been said about *Cane* before Bone published and in the absence of more conclusive evidence than seems to have appeared even until now, Bone's action does seem precipitate, especially in view of some of its consequences.

As not only a Negro novel, but also one of the three best Negro novels, according to the only "old" work dealing with the Negro novel, *Cane* has been acquiring, in the recent years since black literature has become more fashionable than it previously was, what might well be designated as the beginning of a sacred canon. Not unnaturally, when the form and shape of *Cane* are contemplated, in context with the human tendency to exalt *expertise,* a form and shape, that is, which require of any explicator at least a little ingenuity to demonstrate that *Cane* is an organic whole, an attractive article of faith in this sacred canon has been the observeration that *Cane*—although *sans* some of the traditional trappings of a unified piece of long fiction, such as a protagonist and a plot—is nevertheless a novel. In one recent issue of the *CLA Journal,* for example, Bernard Bell undertakes to show how the poems in *Cane*

13. Darwin Turner, "Jean Toomer's *Cane,*" *Negro Digest,* XVIII (January, 1969), 54.
14. Robert Bone, *The Negro Novel in America* (New Haven, Conn., 1958), 81.

operate to give the whole book a functional unity[15] and Patricia
Chase does likewise with *Cane*'s women.[16] Clearly, indeed, that
Cane's author may have resorted to unusual means of compos-
ing a novel is altogether possible. He may even, for that matter,
have resorted to such means without being aware, either in
whole or in part, of what he was doing. Art is full of instances
in which an artist accomplishes more, as well as less, than he
intended. Yet, in reference to *Cane* and its form, some of the
means currently in use to argue for its novelistic identity reflect conceptualizations that can hardly be said to have been in
existence in the 1920s. There is a theory of the absurd, for
instance, inherent in Patricia Chase's description of *Cane*'s
women which, as Miss Chase herself goes to some pains to insist, relates *Cane* to existentialism. And in "Jean Toomer's
Cane" — while specifying that "the form of *Cane* suggests the
kind of breadth and complexity that is in the novel [note the
word *novel*]," and while also apparently acceding to Darwin
Turner's explanation that *Cane* grew from "pieces of shorter
fiction . . . not originally written as parts of a novel" — James
Kraft, author of this article, maintains that "emphasis cannot
. . . be placed upon the form as an original conception." Alluding to an article in *Negro Digest* (July, 1969), wherein Melvin
Dixon characterizes a new black aesthetic as a phenomenon
demanding "an organic, self-creating unity of forms" in which
the black writer discovers his form in the process of creating
it, Kraft goes on to an anatomizing of *Cane* which, dependent
as it is upon a connection with this new black aesthetic, permits
Kraft thus to say: "If it is thought that in the black aesthetic
unity is organic, or self-creating, then the formal unity of *Cane*
as a novel is not affected by Toomer's not originally conceiving
of the parts as forming a whole." [17]

Fifty years ago when *Cane* was composed, Toomer, what-

15. Bernard Bell, "A Key to the Poems in *Cane*," *CLA Journal.* XIV (March, 1971),
251–58.
16. Patricia Chase, "The Women in *Cane*," *CLA Journal*, XIV (March, 1971),
259–73.
17. James Kraft, "Jean Toomer's Cane," *Markham Review*, II (October, 1970), 62.

ever his intentions, could not have been thinking, at least not in doctrinaire terms, of an existentialist theory of the absurd or of a black aesthetic. Two of his far-from-obscure contemporaries, however, Waldo Frank and Gorham Munson, both of whom happened to be white, as well as friends of his, and neither of whom was apparently insensitive to the form of *Cane,* whether it was the result of a deliberate design or of an organic growth, did comment upon the total effect of the book. Neither of them, incidentally, ever refers explicitly to *Cane* as a novel. Waldo Frank, as has been indicated, wrote a foreword for *Cane.* In that foreword he conceived of *Cane* as a "chaos" of verse, tale, and drama, but he also detected in the book a "rhythmic rolling shift" from lyricism to narrative, as from mystery to infinite pathos. It was his view that, carefully read, in *Cane* a "complex and significant form" does take substance from the chaos, a form which, to repeat his direct quotation by Montgomery Gregory, he saw as an "aesthetic equivalent" for the South. For, actually, Frank was more anxious, in his foreword, to emancipate Toomer from a race and a region than he was to do anything else. He insisted that Toomer was primarily a poet, even a poet in prose; and he clearly thought of Toomer's poetic gift as lyric, not epic — not, that is, as the equipment of an artist with a novelist's sense of life or of aesthetic forms. But, still, it was against the possible idea that *Cane* was just a Negro book, or merely a bit of the South in exclusively parochial terms, that Frank was inveighing.

Gorham Munson's appraisal of *Cane* appeared in *Opportunity* in September, 1925, in an article entitled "The Significance of Jean Toomer." Of *Cane*'s form Munson says:

Cane is, from one point of view, the record of his [Toomer's] search for suitable literary forms. We can see him seeking guidance and in several of the stories, notably *Fern* and *Avery,* it is the hand of Sherwood Anderson that he takes hold. But Anderson leads toward formlessness and Toomer shakes him off for Waldo Frank in such pieces as *Theatre* where the design becomes clear and the parts are held in a vital aesthetic union. Finally he breaks through in a free dramatic form of his own, the play *Kabnis* which still awaits production by an

American theatre that cries for good native drama and yet lacks the wit to perceive the talent of Toomer.[18]

It cannot be persuasively argued, therefore, that Munson thought of *Cane* as a novel. Indeed, it would seem rather clear that he thought of it quite otherwise, as a work in which the separate parts displayed a variety of forms. But it can be argued — and this is of some moment — when all of Munson's appraisal of *Cane* is taken into account, that Munson, who does after all speak of the *significance* of Jean Toomer, like Waldo Frank, is much more interested in demonstrating that Toomer had transcended race than in making any other point. Munson's references to Sherwood Anderson and Waldo Frank, or to a native drama for an American theater, are, in themselves incompatible with a black aesthetic. But in the concluding statement of his remarks about *Cane* — and, therefore, about Toomer — Munson arrives at the contention which is truly his prime concern. In this concluding statement, he argues that Toomer has divined the chaos of the modern world and understood that the great categorical imperative for the modern artist is to determine his own proper reaction to that chaos. For Munson, that is, as for Waldo Frank, Toomer was supremely, and superbly, the artist, and universally so, using whatever might be particular in who he was and what he had experienced to render less abstract any of our abstract conceptions of all humankind.

Jean Toomer cannot be dismissed as a writer of no relevance to Negro literature. *Cane*, certainly at this moment, should hardly be dismissed as a work that is clearly not a novel. Nor should any of the present critical activity in connection with *Cane* necessarily be either discouraged or summarily decided. Much of it, I would readily contend, adds to our enjoyment, and our fuller comprehension, of a work well worth the time and effort which a host of explicators may elect to spend upon it. But it may well be all too apparent that the

18. Gorham Munson, "The Significance of Jean Toomer," *Opportunity*, III (September, 1925), 262.

present relation of critical scholarship to *Cane* only illustrates a state of affairs still too endemic in the treatment of Negro literature. For the serious study of literature demands always a due regard for the services of literary history. There are always matters of fact, dry as dust as some of them may superficially seem, which literary critics need to have in their firm possession before they begin their own labors of analysis and appreciation. Everything, for example, about the form of *Cane* would not necessarily be altogether settled if we could speak with reasonable assurance of Toomer's own declared intentions. But knowing those intentions would help. It has been rumored that Toomer once indicated to his publishers that *Cane* was a novel. If he did so, it does not yet appear from a search, supervised by Mrs. Ann Allen Shockley, Associate Librarian and Head of Special Collections for the Fisk University Library, of the more than thirty thousand manuscript pages of Toomer materials in the Toomer Collection. It does appear that Toomer did write at least three works which he presented explicitly as novels: "The Gallonwerps," (1927) "Transatlantic," (1930) and "Eight-Day World" (1932). None of them was ever published, but, apparently, only because he found no publisher willing to accept any of them. There is at least a suggestion in this probable circumstance that Toomer may have lacked the very sense of form that some publishers, or publishers' agents, believed a novelist should have. To start, just on the assumption that *Cane* is a novel (a new kind, of course), and that Toomer intended it so, and then to spin out these theories about his superb sense of organization, may, of course, end up doing no harm. And it is still too early to begin to say too conclusively that *Cane* is not a novel. But it is also, probably even more, too early to say that it is, and surely much too early to pass on from such an exposed position to some of the larger claims, either about the nature of Toomer's art or the relation of that art to the Negro in America, which already, howsoever in the name of sweetness and of light, have been made.

A Survey Course
in Negro
Literature

THE NEED *for some basic agreements in the teaching of Negro literature seems more crucial than ever to me at the present moment. I have delivered the following essay as a lecture in more than one place, and it has recently been published by* College English.

⊱⊰

When I first went to Chapel Hill in 1969 I still affected the luxury of a permissive attitude toward the compulsory study of Negro literature. "Subject Negro literature," I allowed myself to say then, "to the competition of the marketplace." I have changed, if only because, as Langston Hughes once said in another context, the Negro is no longer in vogue. Now I preach that every English major should be required to take a comprehensive general course in Negro literature. I preach also that no American should be granted a bachelor's degree who has not acquired credit for either a general course in Negro literature or a general course in Negro history.

Insofar as we know now, Negro literature begins with a poem called "Bars Fight," which was written in 1746 by a sixteen-year-old girl named Lucy Terry, though it was not published until 1893. The survey of Negro literature which I advocate begins with Lucy Terry and is divided into six periods.

Its first period extends from 1746 until 1830, the year in which David Walker, after preparing the third edition of his famous *Appeal,* met his sudden death on a Boston street, possibly by assassination. I call this period the "Apprentice Years." My second period extends from 1830 through 1895. Perhaps the most convenient date in all of Negro history, 1895 is the year in which—I am giving the actual order of events— first, Frederick Douglass died at his fine residence in Anacostia after he had returned home from being honored at one meeting and just as he was preparing to go on to another public honoring while, only a few weeks later, Booker T. Washington, at the Cotton States Exposition in Atlanta, was to deliver the historic speech in which he assured the white South that in all things purely social, Negroes and whites could be as separate as the fingers, yet one as the hand in all things, as he put it, essential to mutual progress. This second period of sixty-five years I call the "Age of the Abolitionists." My third period extends from 1895 until 1920. The symbols of its great dichotomy are Washington and the relatively young W. E. B. DuBois of the doctrine of the "Talented Tenth." I call this period the "Negro Nadir." My fourth period is the "Harlem Renaissance." It is virtually coterminous with the 1920s, but with a dying fall into the beginning of the 1930s. My fifth period I call the "Age of Wright," for I contend that Richard Wright dominated it as no other Negro writer has ever dominated Negro letters. This period extends from the early 1930s until 1957—until after, that is, Rosa Parks refused to move in Montgomery. My sixth and final period is the period of the "Black Militants," from about 1957 until now, the 1970s.

Apprentice Years

In my first period four poets—Lucy Terry, Jupiter Hammon, Phillis Wheatley, and George Moses Horton—occupy a stage shared with the writers of prose narratives—Briton Hammon, John Marrant, and Olaudah Equiano—and with early Negro leaders whose presence in a course in Negro literature, during the initiatory stages of the course, is highly important if the leaders are used, as they should be, to remind students, many of whom have been accustomed to expect Negro talent only in the exploits of "exceptional" Negroes, that the American Negro, even as early as the formative years of his American identity, began then to build, for his own self-respect, his own communal institutions. So this first period should not ignore Richard Allen, founder and first bishop of the AME Church, who is sometimes called the Father of Black America; Prince Hall, founder of the Negro Masons, the first Negro fraternal order (lodges have meant much in Negro life); Benjamin Banneker, who sounded a note connecting him with Negro higher education; John Russwurm, cofounder of the Negro press; the leading pioneer Negro business man, James Forten; the integrationist, Lemuel Haynes; the colonizationist, Paul Cuffe; and Peter Williams, pastor of a Negro congregation in a white denominational church. Each of these leaders, incidentally, did write something.

Age of the Abolitionists

My second period of Negro literature is preeminently the period of the slave narrative, although the first slave narrative was written, or recorded, by a white man over forty years before "Bars Fight" and the last, well into the twentieth century. But the slave narrative is of such importance in Negro literature that no limitations other than those imposed by the chronology of a realistically organized teaching schedule should be observed in handling it. The two big names of this second period are Frederick Douglass and William Wells Brown. Increasingly, the classic qualities of Douglass' *Narrative of Frederick Douglass, An American Slave, Written by Himself* are being proclaimed. Brown wrote the first Negro novel and the first Negro play. In the shadow of the slave narrative, and of Douglass and of Brown, stand Frances Ellen Watkins Harper, poet, novelist, and short-story writer, and poet Albery

Whitman, whose *Not a Man and Yet a Man* is not the longest poem written by a Negro, but whose stature as a figure of some eminence in Negro literature may now be steadily increasing in the judgment of informed observers. Quick reference in this period should be made to the poets, Charles Reason, George Boyer Vashon, James M. Whitfield, and James Madison Bell, and to the historian, George Washington Williams.

Negro Nadir

Intelligent orchestration of the period of the "Negro Nadir" would seem to require that Charles W. Chesnutt be paired with Paul Laurence Dunbar, and Washington with his fiery opposite, DuBois. Nevertheless, DuBois' whole long, almost seventy-year career, which includes the Black Fame trilogy written long after Washington had been gathered to his forebears, probably should be presented as a unit. The Negro dialect poets, James Edwin Campbell, Daniel Webster Davis, James David Corrothers, and J. Mord Allen, moreover, may be introduced with Dunbar. A small outpouring of very bad novels, woefully similar in their crudities and their simpering gentilities, as much as any other single combined effect, provides a character to this period. These novels can easily be disposed of *en masse*, although, even so, perhaps best with some detailed attention to Elbert Sutton Griggs, who wrote, published, and peddled with his own hand, five of these unhappy artifacts in less than ten years. Other writers of this period— the poets William Stanley Braithwaite, Georgia Douglass Johnson, and the Cotters, father and son, and the short-story writers George Marion McClellan (also a poet), James McGirt, the elder Cotter, and Dunbar's wife, Alice Moore Dunbar Nelson—deserve only passing mention. Fenton Johnson, poet and short-story writer, leads into the Harlem Renaissance. Even more does James Weldon Johnson, who, in his spanning of generations, should, like DuBois, be treated as a unit, but whose novel, *The Autobiography of an Ex-Coloured Man,* is a major work of the "Negro Nadir."

Harlem Renaissance

The writers of the Harlem Renaissance, as Negro writers go, tend to be well known. I shall not linger over them. This is the period of Jean Toomer, Claude McKay, Countee Cullen, the younger Langston Hughes, and the younger Arna Bontemps, the much-too-ignored Anne Spencer, the later James Weldon Johnson and the midpassage DuBois (both of whom should have already, in this course, received their due), Frank Horne, Gwendolyn Bennett, Helene Johnson, and, primarily as novelists, Jessie Redmon Fauset, Wallace Thurman, Rudolph Fisher, George Schuyler, Walter White, Nella Larsen, and Zora Neale Hurston. McKay, Cullen, and Hughes, lyricists all, are the poets' triumvirate of this period. Perhaps the individual works of prose fiction to be stressed are Toomer's *Cane,* McKay's *Home to Harlem,* Cullen's *One Way to Heaven,* Hughes's *Not Without Laughter,* Bontemps' *God Sends Sunday,* Fauset's *Comedy: American Style,* Thurman's *The Blacker the Berry,* Fisher's *The Walls of Jericho,* Schuyler's *Black No More,* and Larsen's *Quicksand.* But the Harlem Renaissance possesses a unifying theme—the "New Negro"—and in this theme it rejects both the "darky" of American minstrelsy, the ebon beast of *The Birth of a Nation,* and the "dicty" of the bad novels of the "Negro Nadir." Not until black militancy would Negro literature be so dedicated in its adherence to a theme and so consciously loyal to a program correlated with that theme. Most of the participants in the Harlem Renaissance were young at the time of Renaissance. Arna Bontemps is still active. Of Langston Hughes no presentation would be just which did not reflect the length and versatility of his career, as well as his sympathetic sensitivity to the changes in atmosphere and *zeitgeist* around him. Nor would such a presentation be just if it failed to establish Hughes as a figure of the first magnitude in Negro literary history. He is not our greatest Negro writer. He may, nevertheless, be our greatest Negro writing man.

Age of Wright

The "Age of Wright," whatever the future may hold, is, until now, the golden age of Negro literature. For all of its high spirits and genuine desire to present the Negro, new or old, as he actually was, the Harlem Renaissance was guilty of its own method of misrepresenting Negroes. In both prose and poetry the Renaissance tended too often to turn Negro life into too much of a myth and a fairy tale. There was something unreal, something superficial, something that was too arch and studied, upon occasion, in the Renaissance version of Negro life. But the "Age of Wright" built upon what was solid in the Renaissance even as it reconstructed it and brought it closer to reality. Moreover, for this later age, apparently, its sense of realism, as well as of reality, was honed into fine focus by the asperities of the Great Depression. The added vision and power of the writers of this age announce themselves early in the poetry of Sterling Brown and Frank Marshall Davis, surely the two most incredibly neglected of all Negro poets. In Brown's *Southern Road* and in a poem like Davis' "Snapshots of the Cotton South," Renaissance pastiche largely disappears. With increments of precious meaning the world which has produced the black peasantry of the sharecropping South, the Negro migrant of the urban slum, and the precarious Negro middle class of both North and South is brought into sounder artistic focus. For Brown and Davis are not only rather accurate sociopolitical observers, they are also true poets.

The greatest writer of this age, however, is Richard Wright, and, if not Wright, Ralph Ellison; and if the pinnacle of achievement in Negro literature until now has not been reached by these two, then it has been reached by one, or all, of the three poets, Melvin Tolson, Robert Hayden, and Pulitzer prize-winning Gwendolyn Brooks, through the poetry which this trio wrote during the "Age of Wright." Study of this period, as of a comprehensive course in Negro literature, climaxes in a study of these five. Even so, the "Age of Wright" probably is still inadequately treated unless some reference is made therein at least to poets Owen Dodson, Margaret Walker, and M. Carl Holman, to novelists Chester Himes, Ann Petry, William Gardner Smith, and John Oliver Killens in *Youngblood,* and to James Baldwin in his essays and fiction before *Another Country.* Baldwin is a writer of whom much must be said. *Another Country,* for example, belongs to the "Age of Wright," and yet it does not. It is truly a protest novel, written as much to commiserate with whites as with blacks.

Black Militants

But there is little commiseration for whites in the poetry, prose, and drama of the black militant, the prevailing Negro writer of the present age. More Negro writers are being published now than ever before. Clearly, the leading militant is Leroi Jones, or Imamu Amiri Baraka, as he prefers to be called. Through Baraka's contributions to the drama, however, it may be expedient to review the history of the American Negro as playwright and as a creator for the American stage. Baraka's poetry is a door to the introduction of other black militant poets, particularly Don L. Lee. But the list of currently active black poets is long, and practical considerations demand a somewhat stringent selection among them for classroom use. Of current novelists perhaps John A. Williams, Paule Marshall, William Demby, William Melvin Kelley, and Ernest Gaines should be treated in some detail. Of current novels surely reference must be made at least to Williams' *The Man Who Cried I Am,* Marshall's *The Chosen Place, The Timeless People,* Demby's *The Catacombs,* Kelley's *A Different Drummer* and *Dem,* and Gaines's *The Autobiography of Miss Jane Pittman.* But, again, the current black novels and novelists are sufficiently numerous to render stringent selection among them a categorical imperative. Moreover, it would certainly appear that no review of the current activity in Negro literature can be respectable which does not include analyses of Eldridge Cleaver's *Soul on Ice*, of *The Autobiography of Malcolm X*, and such other autobiographical works as those of Claude Brown and Piri Thomas.

A special word of caution, incidentally, may be needed about this period. It is preeminently the period of the black militant. Yet it is far from that exclusively. No formula derived exclusively from the thought of Frantz Fanon and the religion of black separatism will fit in any way, for example, Margaret Walker's novel *Jubilee* or Demby's *The Catacombs* or even Claude Brown's *Manchild in the Promised Land.* Finally, Negroes are still writing short stories, as witness James McPherson and Cyrus Coulter; and in the detective novels of Chester Himes, the science fiction of Samual Delany, and the costume romances of Frank Yerby (whose *Speak Now* seems to be an attempt to revive within his product the serious outlook of his early short story "Health Card"), the Negro writer does essay (as did, earlier, Negro writer Willard Motley in his novels *Knock on Any Door* and *They Fished All Night*) other voices and other rooms beyond those usually associated with Negro literature.

It well may be that more emphasis should be put, in teaching a general course in Negro literature, on a reserve shelf than is generally the case. The shelf need not, and probably should not, be large. But almost brutal tactics should be employed to insure its use. Ideally, several copies of every reserve book should on the reserve shelf. Moreover, it is background in Negro history rather than criticism of Negro literature which the reserve shelf should emphasize. I recommend as follows: for Negro history, as a reference to be used throughout the course, John Hope Franklin's *From Slavery to Freedom;* as an account of the African slave trade, Malcolm Cowley and Daniel Mannix's *Black Cargoes;* to put the case for African survivals in the Americas, Melvile Herskovits' *The Myth of the Negro Past;* to picture the history of the Negro family, and also to argue against Herskovits, E. Franklin Frazier's *The Negro Family in the United States;* as an introduction to the Negro leadership of accommodation and the Negro leadership of protest, chapters 33 through 37 of Gunnar Myrdal's *An American Dilemma;* as a background for the Harlem Renaissance, Nathan Huggins' *The Harlem Renaissance;* to prepare the student for the ghetto, Sinclair Drake and Horace Cayton's *Black Metropolis;* as a prelude to the current scene, Louis Lomax's *The Negro Revolt;* and, as a stimulant to consider black psychology, William H. Grier and Price M. Cobbs's *Black Rage.* Reference works on the reserve shelf to be consulted as the title indicates might well include Vernon Loggins' *The Negro Author: His Development in America to 1900;* J. Saunders Redding's *To Make a Poet Black;* Hugh Gloster's *Negro Voices in American Fiction;* Robert Bone's *The Negro Novel in America;* David Littlejohn's *Black on White;* Edward Margolies' *Native Sons: A Critical Study of Twentieth-Century Negro American Authors; Black Expression* and *The Black Aesthetic,* two collections of essays both edited by Addison Gayle; and, though they may well have other uses, Harold Cruse's *The Crisis of the Negro Intellectual* and Frantz Fanon's *The Wretched of the Earth.*

The text for this course now can be an anthology. It is not for me to choose among those currently available. But I would close with a statement about the teacher of the course. Whoever teaches it should continue to teach it for years, if not for life. I have said nothing here about the still relative dearth of extensive research in Negro literary history. I do say here that this dearth is somewhat matched by a lack of familiarity, on the part of many teachers of Negro literature, with the actual total corpus of Negro writing. At the moment only repeated teaching of a truly comprehensive course in Negro literature can overcome for most recruits to Negro literature this lack of familiarity. By accretion—the repeated reading for class presentation of, for example, John Marrant's *Narrative of the Lord's Wonderful Dealings with John Marrant, a Black,* David Walker's *Appeal,* William Wells Brown's *Clotel* in its several versions, the long poems of Albery Whitman, some of the bad novels of the early 1900s,

poems like Dunbar's "The Haunted Oak," James Weldon Johnson's "St. Peter Relates an Incident of the Judgement Day,"
Countee Cullen's "Heritage," Sterling Brown's "Black Odys-
sey," Gwendolyn Brooks's "Satin-Legs Smith," and Imamu Baraka's "Jitterbugs," as well as of numerous other novels, shorter
pieces of fiction and poetry and plays—a literature does grow
into the consciousness of those who would teach it. By such an
accretion one does acquire a sense, not only of individual writers and works, but also of the shape and organic nature of an
integrated literary tradition.

And Negro literature is an integrated literary tradition. It
does have its continuities, its new departures, its interaction
with a world of human experience, and its own interpretations
of its own underlying epistemologies. Moreover, it is not devoid
of art. All courses in literature are, or should be, courses in
life. But the attention to art in them makes of them more than
courses in social science. It makes of them courses in the
humanities. By accretion, every general survey course in Negro
literature should, I think, become a course in the humanities. I
have argued a compulsory degree-requirement in either Negro
history or Negro literature. I further argue that a general
course in Negro literature should offer more than a course in
Negro history. I argue that it should become, in any fair competition between history and literature, the preferred alter-
native. I argue that, with increasing knowledge of the literary
history of Negro literature and increasing insight into the art
that often does accompany the product of the Negro writer, a
good comprehensive survey course in Negro literature will
become a course in the humanities. And I argue that this is
precisely what such a course should become. And I argue that,
otherwise, it has little, if any, reason for inclusion in any college
curriculum. For otherwise, it fails to serve, not only the interest
of the specialist, but also the broader, finer interests of all of
those who believe in the parliament of man and the genuine,
though not necessarily governmental, federation of the world.

Index